THE ROMANOVS' MURDER CASE

The Myth of the Basement Room Massacre

T. G. Bolen

abbott press

Abbott Press books may be ordered through booksellers or by contacting:

Abbott Press
1663 Liberty Drive
Bloomington, IN 47403
www.abbottpress.com
Phone: 1 (866) 697-5310

ISBN: 978-1-4582-2183-4 (sc)
ISBN: 978-1-4582-2182-7 (hc)
ISBN: 978-1-4582-2181-0 (e)

Library of Congress Control Number: 2018907268

Print information available on the last page.

Abbott Press rev. date: 06/26/2018

This book is dedicated to the memory of
Colonel Homer H. Slaughter,
soldier, diplomat, patriot

CONTENTS

AUTHOR'S NOTES

I began writing a seven or eight page article on an aspect of the Romanov murder case. Six years later, this book is the result. Once the Romanov story takes hold with you, escape is impossible. Why do I feel this book might have something to contribute to the Romanov literature?

After graduating from law school, I spent the next four years in a state prosecutor's office trying criminal cases. For four years after that, I defended criminal cases until my practice progressed to the point where I could concentrate in other areas. During the eight years, I read and studied endless police reports. The police can close a case when they feel there is reasonable cause that the suspect committed the crime. For a prosecutor, he has to view the evidence from the point of convincing a jury of the defendant's guilt beyond a reasonable doubt. The two standards are far apart. Therefore, the prosecutor goes over police report in minute detail, not only studying what is there, but looking for what he feels should be there but isn't. I hope that those years of studying crimes and reading police reports might bring a new perspective to the Romanov murders. As in any writing effort, the author will tell you the product is the result of input from a great many people to whom the author owes a great debt of gratitude. For this book there is a long list of people whose assistance and input produce the present volume. In listing them, there are three contributors who have gone above and beyond the call of duty, and I am listing them first. Since there is no distinguishing among the three of them, I have taken the usual course of listing them alphabetically.

My first debt of sincere gratitude goes to my assistant and secretary, Gloria Frantz. She typed and retyped, assembled and reassembled, chapter after chapter in the book for several years. However, an even greater contribution was the fact that she came to also know everything about the Romanov murders and would continually be able to tell me where I had repeated information or where I had used the wrong name in a story and saved me from endless errors. Without her there would be no book. Needless to say, any errors that remain in the book are mine and mine alone.

The next contributor to the book was more valuable than I am able to state. It is my good friend and next door neighbor, Colonel French L. MacLean, United States Army (Ret.). The Colonel is a successful published author with more than a dozen books dealing primarily with military subjects which are the standard work in that category. The first major contribution French made was telling me after I retired from the law practice that I should attempt writing in order to have a project that would help fill my time. Any writing I have done since is the result of French's advice and encouragement. My thanks to him are never ending. In addition, whenever the project lagged, French was there with assistance and encouragement to keep the book going. More than that, he is responsible for all the material from the National Archives in Maryland and Missouri, where he spent hour after hour researching the Colonel Slaughter story and copying dozens and dozens of documents which he furnished to me for the book. As the book reveals, it was French who took the photograph of Colonel Slaughter's slide which would show the three sheet wrapped bodies in the upstairs bedroom. He made two 30-hour road trips to examine the slides and take the photographs. This book is as much his as it is mine.

The third group are not only valuable contributors, but an inspiration in the writing of the book. That is the family of Colonel Homer Slaughter. Colonel Slaughter's three sons and two of their wives are deceased, leaving as the only survivor of that generation his daughter-in-law, Mrs. Stephen (Pat) Slaughter. She has been a help and inspiration over the entire preparation of this book. She patiently and courteously answered my phone calls and questions, which frequently went over ground she had answered before. As a living link with Colonel Slaughter, her memories are invaluable. Now in her 90s, her answers to my questions were quick, concise, and accurate as she recalled memories from her past as clearly as if they had happened last week. One of the joys of writing this book has been my association with her, for whom my admiration is boundless. I also owe an acknowledgment to the grandchildren of Colonel Slaughter. In like manner, they answered endlessly my questions and provided a valuable source of family information. I am sure that Colonel Slaughter would be as proud of his family, as they are of him.

In addition, there are others who made extremely valuable contributions to the final edition of the book. I was, indeed, fortunate to have the assistance of Shay McNeal, the author of the book on attempts to rescue the Tsar, which is the standard in its field. Shay not only used her own time to completely read the unpublished text of the book, but page by page noted comments which are reproduced in the finished book. These included not only helpful points from her knowledge of the Romanov family, which saved me from errors, but also made changes in the prose, which made it more reasonable and showed the hand of a professional writer.

A sincere thanks also to Anthony Summers, the co-author of the ground breaking book THE FILE ON THE TSAR. Tony was kind enough to read the manuscript before publication and offer his thoughts on several situations regarding the Romanovs in my draft. Tony and his wife Robbyn Swan raised a number of interesting points which gave me an opportunity to review possible answers. Their help and insight are much appreciated.

Any student who wishes to study the Romanov matter will find that the assistance of the Hoover Institute at Stanford University is a landmark in the study of the issues. Their help was continuous from their unbelievable archives regarding the Romanovs, which was constantly made available to me by the Director of Russian Studies, Dr. Anatol Shmelev. In addition, my favorite researcher, Ron Basich, who does research at the Hoover Institute, provided year after year endless information which he discovered in the institute files. Anyone wishing anything from the Hoover Institute cannot do better than obtain the services of Ron.

The facts in this book are from several sources. Any pictures bearing a Russian title are from the Russian edition of Sokolov's work published by Slowo in Berlin in 1926. Diligent attempts to find anyone holding a copyright with respect to the same were unavailable. The bulk of the remaining pictures are in the public domain, except that a number of the pictures of the Ipatiev House are in the collection of the author. They were taken in 1918 and bear a legend asking that credit for those pictures be given to the American Red Cross in Siberia. The photograph of Colonel Slaughter and the slide of the upstairs bedroom itself are furnished by the kind permission of the Slaughter family.

PROLOGUE

Every fairy tale contains the story of a prince. He is young, handsome, a dutiful son, and a good companion. The story takes him through his life until the time he inherits the throne. The prince becomes the ruler of a huge empire and its millions of people. He lives a life of opulence with everything available that unlimited wealth can furnish. He meets a princess, falls in love, and they become soulmates and enter into a happy marriage. This is stuff of fairy tales, but, in this case, there was such a prince. He was not an ancient pharaoh or a Roman emperor but a man of the twentieth century who received and sent telegrams, owned an automobile, and appeared in motion picture footage. He, in fact, was the total autocrat and richest man in the world, - Nicholas II, Tsar of all the Russias.

Upon his succession to the throne, he was married to Princess Alexandra of Hesse and they remained absolutely devoted to each other for the rest of their lives. The empire spread out before him and the world was at his feet. But for this prince, the ending was different. At age 50, brutally murdered by his subjects, his body was mutilated and thrown into a mass, unmarked grave with eight other persons in a swampy bog in the middle of a remote forest.

This is his story.

PREFACE

The night of July 16, 1918, was moderately warm even in Ekaterinburg. It was also very short, being sandwiched in between two long Siberian summer days, and if conventional wisdom is to be believed, it was also bloody, violent, and tragic, for according to that conventional wisdom, July 16 is the night that Nicholas II, the last reigning Tsar of Russia, his wife, Alexandra, and their five children were murdered in the small basement room of a borrowed house in Ekaterinburg.

Over the years, the account of the night of July 16 would be compared and contrasted to the first definitive account of the murders as was compiled by Nicholas Sokolov,[1] an investigator appointed by the White Russian authorities, who concluded the Romanovs and their attendants were murdered in the Ipatiev basement murder room. Before undertaking this new examination, I must state the debt I owe to the people who have gone before me on this expedition. The first writer to give a serious review of the Sokolov account was John F. O'Conor.[2] His book is the first serious effort that finds fault with the Sokolov conclusions.

Any writer then must also acknowledge the contribution of the authors of *THE FILE ON THE TSAR*.[3] In their landmark book, Anthony Summers and Thomas Mangold challenged Sokolov's account with evidence and precision. As Sokolov's conclusions over the course of six decades became the accepted facts regarding the final end of the Romanovs, Summers and Mangold tirelessly reviewed the old materials with a current criminal analysis by experts and raised questions that provided substantial doubt that the facts the world had accepted as true from Sokolov's account were not only open to question but might well be untrue.

The events of that summer night also receive a critical evaluation and examination in *THE LAST TSAR*[4] by Edvard Radzinsky. In his text, the author not only reviews the existing evidence but adds numerous previously unpublished accounts related to him by Russians who heard the story from relatives and friends of participants, along with a number of previously unknown documents. The highlight in that category is the "Yurovsky Note" which the author discovered in a file in the official Russian records. Yacov Yurovsky was one of the Ekaterinburg Bolsheviks involved with the assassination. In his Note, he claims to have been the head of the execution and burial squad, and that claim had been generally accepted over the years.

The literature received a work on the complete events of the summer of 1918 with regard to Nicholas II, his wife, and children in *THE FATE OF THE ROMANOVS*[5] by Gregory King and Penny Wilson. This volume takes the story to its furthest reaches with documents, testimony, photographs, and conclusions to a degree not available before the publication of this work. In *THE SECRET PLOT TO SAVE THE TSAR*,[6] Shay McNeal uncovers numerous facts made by Allied efforts. This well written, scholarly book is a must read for Romanov students. It destroys completely the idea that King George V did not make any effort to rescue his Romanov relatives. A look at the Romanov individuals themselves is set forth in a work by Helen Rappaport. Her book, *THE ROMANOV SISTERS*,[7] is a discussion of the daughters themselves and their lives as they became adults.

INTRODUCTION

THE ROMANOV DYNASTY

The Romanov Dynasty had ruled Russia for over 300 years at the time of its overthrow. The first Romanov Tsar, Michael, was chosen in 1613 when there was no acknowledged successor to the throne. Over 300 years the Romanovs provided capable, ambitious, brutal, and sometimes insane, rulers to the Russian Empire. By the early nineteenth century, there were few Romanovs left in Russia, and many people questioned whether those few Romanovs were actually of legitimate Imperial blood. Nevertheless, on the death of Alexander I in 1879, Nicholas I, the Iron Tsar, became the absolute autocrat of Russia. The Romanov Grand Dukes who lived during the nineteenth and twentieth century were descendants of Nicholas I. His eldest son, Alexander II, followed him on the throne, ruling until murdered by a terrorist bomb in 1881. Alexander II had three younger brothers, the Grand Duke Konstantin, the Grand Duke Nicholas, and the Grand Duke Michael. These four brothers produced 16 adult sons, thus adding to the number of Imperial Grand Dukes.

Under the statute laid down in 1797 by the mentally defective Paul I, the crown could pass only to male heirs and the male descendants of male heirs. Although this decree would seem to have been obviously amendable or voidable by his successors, who were the absolute lawgivers during their reigns, they continually honored Paul's dictum, and female descendants became outcasts outside the line of Imperial succession.

Alexander II was the father of six sons, the eldest of whom, Nicholas, would have been heir to the throne had not his untimely death occurred in his 20's, which moved his next oldest brother, Alexander, to the front of the line of succession, as well as becoming the new fiancé and later the husband of the deceased brother's intended bride, Princess Dagmar of Denmark.

The male children of Tsar Alexander III were his three sons who lived into adulthood: Nicholas II, who would be his successor; Grand Duke George, who died in his late 20's from tuberculosis never having married; and Grand Duke Michael, who married morganatically[8] perhaps the most notorious woman in Russia, the twice divorced Natalie Wulfert,[9] the ex-wife of a Moscow musician, as well as the present wife of a guard's officer serving in Grand Duke Michael's regiment. Nicholas II's only male heir, Tsareveich Alexei, was found a few weeks after his birth to be a hemophiliac.

In the early twentieth century, the life of a hemophiliac was understood to be filled with danger and almost always short. Hemophilia, which causes the failure of the blood to clot, was known as the royal disease since it was believed to have been transmitted through Alexei's mother, the Empress Alexandra, from her grandmother, Queen Victoria of England, who apparently was the first carrier in the English royal family. Victoria gave birth to one hemophiliac son, Prince Leopold, Duke of Albany, whose daughter also gave birth to a hemophiliac son. Queen Victoria's second daughter, Princess Alice of Hesse, Empress Alexandra's mother, also gave birth to a hemophiliac son who died at a very early age from a fall. Princess Alice's daughters, Alex of Hesse and Irene of Hesse, both gave birth to hemophiliac sons. Hemophilia also descended in the line of Victoria's daughter, Beatrice, and through her to her daughter, Ena, the Queen of Spain, and then to Ena's sons, and it also affected the two Battenberg sons of Beatrice.

Thus, when Nicholas and Alexandra saw the fatal trickle of blood from their infant son's navel, they knew the terrible fate that awaited their family. In order that no one should realize that the heir to the Russian throne suffered from a life-threatening disease, Nicholas and Alexandra kept the secret to themselves, not even revealing it to their siblings. This effort to conceal Alexei's condition began to give rise to many current rumors about his condition. For this reason, at the time of Nicholas's abdication and for the 13 years before, the death of the heir, Tsareveich Alexei, hovered as a constant possibility.

This made the succession to the throne after Alexei vest in the descendants in the male line of Nicholas II's grandfather, Alexander II, and after that, through the descendants in the male line of Alexander II's next oldest brother. The importance of this line of descent will become obvious when we later reach the point of the 1918 murders at Alpayevsk.

Alpayevsk, a small town close to Ekaterinburg, is where a group of Romanovs were being held. These included Grand Duchess Elizabeth, who was the widow of Grand Duke Serge Alexandrovich and also a sister of the Empress Alexandra; Grand Duke Serge Mikhialovich; the three sons of Grand Duke Konstantin (always known as KR) who were princes of the royal blood; along with Prince Paley, the son of a morganatic marriage of Grand Duke Paul Alexandrovich, all of whom were killed by the Bolsheviks by being thrown down a 60 foot mine shaft on the night of July 17, 1918. Alexander II's four other sons produced a small number of male heirs.

The next brother, Grand Duke Vladimir, had three sons who, with their father, would have been next in line of succession after Alexander III if he had no descendants in the male line. Grand Duke Vladimir's right to the throne and that of his descendants, however, had a serious flaw. To be crowned a Russian Tsar, one must have married in a Russian Orthodox ceremony an Orthodox bride who was of royal birth. Vladimir had married Marie,[10] a German princess, who remained a Lutheran for many years after their marriage. Construed strictly, this would have removed Vladimir from the succession, as well as his sons.

The oldest son, Grand Duke Kyril, had an additional infirmity in that he married his first cousin, Victoria Melita, which was forbidden by the Russian Orthodox Church, and further complicated by the fact that she was the divorced ex-wife of the Empress Alexandra's brother, Grand Duke Ernest of Hesse. Kyril was personally unpopular with the rest of the Imperial family and seriously damaged his position when, on the day before Nicholas II abdicated in March 1917, he broke his oath to the Emperor by placing a red cockade on his clothing and marching the military unit under his command to the Duma,[11] which was the Russian parliament, to turn them over to the command of the provisional government. Although Kyril, in exile, claimed to be Emperor during the 1920's, his claim was honored by very few members of the dynasty. Kyril's two brothers, Andrew and Boris, were not considered to be Emperor material by anyone, including themselves.

The next sons of Alexander II in line were Grand Duke Alexei, who died in 1908, never having married, and the fifth son, Grand Duke Serge, married Empress Alexandra's sister, Elizabeth of Hesse. The strong belief was that the marriage was never consummated, and Serge left no surviving descendants. Finally, the youngest brother, Grand Duke Paul, had married in accordance with the requirements of Russian law, marrying in an Orthodox ceremony, the Orthodox Royal Princess Alexandra of Greece. This marriage produced one son, Grand Duke Dmitri, but the Grand Duchess Alexandra died giving birth to her son. Grand Duke Paul subsequently married a divorced commoner, which eliminated his claim to the throne. This left his son, the Grand Duke Dmitri, a grandson of Alexander II, in the male line as the person with the best claim of succession. Unfortunately, the problem with Dmitri as Tsar was that he was an alleged co-conspirator in the cold blooded murder of Rasputin in December 1916. It is difficult to think that the Russian people would have accepted as their Tsar, whom they believed to be the anointed of God, a man who participated in a premeditated, gory murder.

This situation meant that the succession would leave the descendants of Alexander II and go to the descendants of the next oldest brother, Grand Duke Konstantin. The son, KR, would die shortly before the succession question arose. His other son, Grand Duke Dmitri, would be murdered by the Bolsheviks in January 1919 never having married and leaving no surviving descendants.

Consequently, the next in the line of succession are the Romanov princes of the royal blood who are the sons of KR. The oldest, Prince Ioan, was a popular choice as he was married to Princes Helen, the daughter of the King of Serbia, and they already had a son. There was a slight problem with the religion of the wife of KR which could have removed them from the succession.

If that were the case, the line would pass to the descendants of Alexander II's second oldest brother, Grand Duke Nicholas. He had two sons, the oldest son being another Grand Duke Nicholas who would die leaving no descendants, and the second son, Grand Duke Peter, who had a son, Prince Roman, who had no question at all regarding the line of succession. The only difficulty with Prince Roman is that he was Nicholas II's great grandfather's great grandson, being the son of the second son of the third son of Nicholas I. If the key to monarchy is its heredity succession, this does a fair amount of violence to the theory.

What then brings us to the point where the Imperial Romanov Dynasty after 300 years of ruling Russia and its last Tsar, a complete autocrat and "God's anointed," can be overthrown in a matter of days, starting their country down a path which will result in the cold blooded murder of the Tsar, his wife, their children, and half of the entire Imperial family? This rain cloud had been growing larger on the horizon for many years. Nicholas's grandfather, Alexander II, the Tsar who freed the serfs in 1861, two years before Lincoln emancipated the slaves, explained as his reason for doing so was that when revolution came, it was better that it came from the top down rather than the bottom up. Alexander II, the Tsar liberator, was riding in his carriage on a Sunday morning in 1881 after an Imperial dress parade when a terrorist rolled a bomb to his carriage. With the aim that was common among terrorists, he managed to kill one of the Cossack escorts and a horse. Instead of speeding from the scene, Alexander II stepped from his coach and went to attend to the fatally wounded Cossack. At this point, a second terrorist standing a few feet away with a second bomb simply rolled it to the Tsar's feet where it exploded, shredding one leg and blowing off the other, lacerating his face and tearing a large wound in his abdomen. The Tsar was hastily driven back to the palace, but he had only approximately two hours of life left.

Alexander III, who succeeded his father, thus came to the throne with the understanding that only harsh punishments, imprisonment, and executions would stem the revolutionary tide in Russia. The net effect, of course, was just the opposite. Assassinations would continue with Alexander III's younger brother, Grand Duke Serge, being blown to death in 1905 by another terrorist bomb thrown under his carriage in an explosion so fierce that a finger found on an adjoining building was essentially the only recognizable part of his body.[12] The members of the Imperial family knew then they lived a life where death could await them around any corner.

A result of this gathering storm was that Nicholas II and his family spent most of their time at their retreat, the Alexander Palace at Tsarskoe Selo about 15 miles from St. Petersburg, not only because the Empress disliked St. Petersburg society and the court, but because it was considered safer than their appearing in the streets of St. Petersburg. At Tsarskoe Selo, the Tsar and his family thought they could essentially live a quiet secluded life surrounded by guards and assure that Alexei's true affliction would be kept from the public eye.

THE BEGINNING OF THE END OF THE DYNASTY

The spark that would light the fire and subsequently burn the Romanovs' shaky throne to the ground was the Great War, which started in August 1914. The purpose here is not to go into the causes of the Great War, the subject which has already occupied volume after volume of Russian history, but to discuss the cause of the start of hostilities as the same relates to the action of Nicholas II and then the effect that the war itself had on Nicholas II and the dynasty. Fate played an unhappy trick on the world in 1914 with respect to the rulers of Russia, Germany, Austria, and England. Three were absolute monarchies and the fourth a constitutional monarchy. Three of the then monarchs had succeeded their fathers, all of whom would have taken every opportunity to avoid a general European war. Nicholas's father, Alexander III, was well known for his adversity to any kind of armed conflict. Alexander III would have exercised every bit of his forceful personality and ability to avoid the conflict. In the same way, Kaiser Wilhelm II, also an absolute monarch, succeeded his father, Kaiser Frederick Wilhelm, who was indoctrinated in the art of liberal educated ruling by both his wife, Princess Victoria of Britain, and her father, the German born Albert, Prince Consort and husband of Queen Victoria of Britain. Kaiser Wilhelm II's father died after only 99 days on the throne from a terrible cancer of the throat. Nicholas II's father died at the early age of 49 and, therefore, would easily have been on the throne in 1914 had he lived. The constitutional monarch, George V of England, had, of course, no absolute power, as did his other two first cousins, the Kaiser and the Tsar, but an abler, more experienced monarch might have been able to calm the passions that arose in July 1914. Had his diplomatic father, the suave Edward VII, still been on the throne, he doubtless would have had more effect on events than did George V. Edward VII died at the age of 70, only four years before the start of the Great War, so he would, had he lived a long life, easily have been on the throne in 1914. Combining these three, perhaps the worst fateful reality was that the fourth throne, Austria-Hungary, was occupied by an absolute monarch, Franz Joseph, who having ruled for 60 years, had long outlived his expectancy on the throne. The Austro-Hungarian government and its general staff knew that Franz Joseph was effectively a dead weight on the top of the crumbling pyramid of the empire. His nephew and heir, Franz Ferdinand, whose assassination helped ignite the war, although not popular, was somewhat more liberal than Franz Joseph and at least would have entered into the deliberations and could not have been less helpful to the cause of peace than Franz Joseph. Thus, the three men on the thrones of Europe who could have helped prevent the catastrophe were dead, and followed by their three less effective sons, while the one emperor who failed to take any constructive action to forestall the catastrophe lived on and on.

There was a reason the Archduke Franz Ferdinand's death resulted in the chaos it did. After Austrian threats against Serbia, the German Kaiser Wilhelm II gave Austria Germany's promised military support, to which Nicholas responded by giving Serbia Russia's backing. The Kaiser and Nicholas both contributed to the incendiary atmosphere by mobilizing their troops along the common border. Nicholas, partly in the control of his general staff, and the Kaiser, partly in the control of his general staff, nevertheless exercised what little independent judgment they used in an unwise manner. Orders by either one to their general staffs could have obtained a delay which, if it did not prevent the war, certainly would not have allowed it to flame into action in the first week of August 1914. Nicholas, as always indecisive and in agreement with the last strong opinion he received, put Russia on a wartime footing. The Kaiser, always egotistic, belligerent, and unintelligent, cooperated in the mistake and, therefore, he and Nicholas together sent their peoples and armies into a collision which would destroy them both.

The tragedy of the war was not only the slaughter of millions of soldiers and innocent civilians but the disasters it brought to many of the ruling families, including the Hohenzollerns of Germany, the Hapsburgs of Austria, and the Romanovs of Russia. Nicholas's fate was the swiftest, primarily because the war was an internal disaster for Russia. At the start of the war, Nicholas enjoyed perhaps his greatest popularity when people patriotically rallied behind the Tsar, who vowed to rid Russian soil of the foreign troops. A great surge of nationalism enveloped Nicholas in August of 1914. By the end of 1914, the patriotic fervor had largely disappeared. The country learned that the government and the senior military officers were noted primarily for inefficiency, inability, and corruption. The Russian army was not ready to fight a twentieth century war. It consisted of huge masses of manpower which were thrown wave after wave against the enemy. During the campaigns on the eastern front of 1914, the Russian army went into action with railroads that couldn't supply them, rifles unworkable or without cartridges, artillery pieces with shells of the wrong caliber, and some men armed with sticks and pitchforks. The Russian military tactics often consisted of rushing huge lines of soldiers against entrenched German machine gun battalions. German officers later told of having required their men to go out in front of the machine guns and clear away the Russian corpses as they became stacked so high that the machine guns did not have a clear field of fire. Five months after the start of the war, at the end of December 1914, the Russian military had suffered one million casualties.[13]

Although at this point public blame rested primarily with the cabinet and the military, some of the shock, horror, and disappointment invariably spilled over on the Tsar. Nicholas perhaps might have been able to avoid some of the repercussions had not he made what must be one of the most disastrous decisions of his reign when he assumed personal command of the army in September 1915, discharging his cousin, Grand Duke Nicholas, known as Nicholasha, who had been commander in chief of the Russian forces and whose commanding physical stature occasioned great respect. Though not a military strategist on the order of some of the Great War generals, Nicholasha, nevertheless, was respected by the army and was an imposing figure and a bulwark to his troops, none of which fit the definition of Tsar Nicholas II as commander in chief. Further, by the time Nicholas assumed the command, only military disasters awaited, with the exception of the Brusilov offensive. These were now blamed on the Tsar personally, and his status as a semi-God fell with each military defeat, until we arrive at March of 1917, at which point there was open rebellion and a call from the Russian Parliament for Nicholas's resignation. At that point there was a chance of Alexei as a successor with a regency, or next the succession of Nicholas's brother, Grand Duke Michael, but by the time Nicholas finally determined that there was a problem and started back from army headquarters to St. Petersburg on March 17, 1917, all hopes of any kind of monarchial solution was gone. Two representatives of the Duma met Nicholas to demand his resignation, and all of Nicholas's generals advised him that the army would not support him personally. When Nicholas found that the army, which he undoubtedly believed to be his great support, had abandoned him, he abdicated, but with the sincere hope that his abdication would help both Russia and the war. He was to find very quickly to his sorrow that neither would be true.

THE ROAD TO EKATERINBURG

Nicholas, throughout his entire adult life, faithfully maintained a diary in which he entered the day's events every evening. The text is closer to a day book than a diary as a large part of it consists of comments about the weather or who visited or a recital of the Tsar's menial activities. On only two occasions did the Tsar make an entry which revealed the passion he felt at that day's events. One was on the day of abdication when he entered in his diary at the closing of that day's journal, "All around me is cowardice, treachery, and deceit."[14] It is estimated that perhaps a majority of the Russian population did not necessarily want to see Nicholas executed, but a huge majority of the population did not want him to return to the throne. One of the problems with the overthrow of Nicholas II was that no one was able to appear as an authentic replacement as long as Nicholas, the "God's anointed," was alive, and no one, including the Imperial family, wanted Nicholas to remain or return as Tsar. For months before the abdication, members of the Imperial family had formed in cliques and groups and had written and addressed Nicholas warning him of the danger which lay ahead for himself and his relatives. As his brother-in-law, Grand Duke Alexander, told the Emperor and Empress, he understood that they were willing to throw themselves over the precipice, but they had no right to take the rest of the family with them.[15] Nicholas and Alexandra remained oblivious to the danger and unbelieving of the warnings. On Nicholas's abdication, Russian rule passed to the provisional government and the Russian Parliament, the Duma. From all appearances, the provisional government had no intention or desire to see Nicholas executed but was willing to have him go in exile wherever he could be accepted. Nicholas, idiotically indifferent to the situation as always, preferred to remain in Russia, feeling that going in exile would dim his chances for a return to the throne, not understanding that there was hardly anyone in the entire empire, including the Imperial family, who desired that result. Consequently, he and his family were placed under effective house arrest at their palace and maintained a fairly normal life until August 1917. Alexander Kerensky,[16] the head of the provisional government, made arrangements to send the Imperial family to Tobolsk in Siberia with the motive of relocating the family in a rural backwater settlement where they would be in far less danger. The time for exile to a foreign country had already passed, and as Kerensky explained to Nicholas, "Now they are after me and next they will be after you."[17] It is doubtful that Nicholas ever fully understood until the final moments of his life the danger in which he and his family lived.

Nicholas and his family were taken by the Bolsheviks to Tobolsk in August 1917, along with their retainers and amenities. Probably no deposed monarch ever went into exile with a larger group of retainers and a more substantial set of belongings than Nicholas II. Tobolsk was reachable by taking a train to Tiumen and then a boat up river to Tobolsk. This reinforces the thought that Kerensky was sending them to a place where reactions against the Imperial family would not be so violent and, perhaps, they would be even treated with civility. They were installed in a large residence which had formerly been the governor's home, and Nicholas apparently settled in comfortably. Tobolsk was a far cry from the Alexander Palace, but it was certainly in no sense of the word a set of jail cells. Nicholas and his family were joined in the house by their personal physician, Dr. Eugene Botkin, the Tsar's valet, the Empress's lady's maid, and other household attendants. When this is compared to French King Louis XVI in the Bastille and England's Charles I in prison, the Romanovs' existence does not seem so harsh a punishment. They were, however, confined to the premises and, after a short while, were not allowed to leave the yard of the house. Nicholas apparently bore all this in stride, being very happy to exercise outside when he could and was utterly baffled when the guards did not reciprocate his attempts at friendship. Although they were not allowed visitors, they had the services of Alexei's physician, Dr. Vladimir Derevenko, who was allowed in on a not infrequent basis and, on several occasions, had services performed by a priest and deacon. It was not their previous life of luxury; however, it is difficult to describe it as severe imprisonment. Yet, a problem did arise when their guards and jailers became friendly and even sympathetic with the Imperial family whom they found to be very ordinary persons, with the exception of the Empress, who always remained haughty and imperious to the very end. It is important that the daughters became friendly with several of the guards. Although they had at the palace only reached the emotional level of 12 year olds, their attentions to and from the guards, which could barely be described as flirting, still indicated that there were probably many nominal party members in Tobolsk who would not have been that upset had the Imperial family been rescued and removed from Russia.

In the meantime, Russia staggered to the end of a bloody war, the moderates in the government lost control to Lenin and Trotsky who returned from the safety of foreign countries to take over the reins of government in October 1917. Lenin quickly made peace with Germany by surrendering a large part of Russia's territory to the Germans and rallied the people to his cause with a slogan of "Bread and Peace." This move to the extreme left, of course, increased the danger for the Romanovs. Whatever sympathy they might have had was nonexistent with the more hardened Bolshevik government which regarded them as an expendable cipher to be used only as a bargaining chip. As a result, by April 1918 plans were made to move the Imperial family once again. The Bolsheviks assigned an officer, Vassily Yakolev,[18] as the officer who would transport the Imperial family from Tobolsk to an undesignated destination in the west, which some of the Romanovs would believe was Moscow.

When officer Yakolev arrived at Tobolsk, he found Alexei in such poor physical condition that the child was completely unable to travel. Yakolev then told Nicholas that he must still leave and, after a heartbreaking family counsel, it was decided that Nicholas, Alexandra, and Maria, their daughter, would leave and Alexei and the other three daughters would remain in Tobolsk until Alexei was able to travel.[19] The threesome, with their attendants, boarded the train at Tiumen;

numerous theories abound as to whether they were headed for another town in Siberia, for trial in Moscow, or for escape via Vladivostok. There still exists no essentially question-proof document which indicates what the plans were for the family. The actual result of the trip was that the train was halted in the town of Ekaterinburg, a violently revolutionary community in the Ural Mountains. Telegrams and statements exist indicating numerous scenarios, including that their safety had been guaranteed by the Ekaterinburg Soviet or that Ekaterinburg took them for the purposes of assassination or that Moscow allowed them to be abducted by the Ekaterinburg Soviet, thereby allowing Lenin to wash his hands of the whole problem. Whatever the truth, Nicholas, Alexandra, and Maria were situated in the house of a displaced mining executive, Ipatiev, which was ominously referred to by the Bolsheviks as "the house of special purpose." In a few weeks, Alexei was able to travel and the family was reunited for the last time in Ekaterinburg. The treatment there was certainly stricter than in Tobolsk, but the house was a decent accommodation, had numerous rooms, and consisted of living quarters and not places of imprisonment, although they were certainly restricted with respect to leaving the premises. Nicholas and his family would remain in the Ipatiev House until the infamous night of July 16, 1918.

THE MURDER ROOM

It is hoped this book will bring together as many sources as possible, including those recently published, to allow the reader to compare facts in one concise text. Where conclusions are drawn that are different from earlier authors, this in no sense should be taken as a criticism of those works. Obviously, this work has the benefit of many facts and documents which were not available to earlier writers. I would adopt Newton's analysis of his discoveries which was that he said if he could see farther than those before him had seen, it was because he stood on the shoulders of giants.

The problem that has vexed students for nearly a century is how were the seven Romanovs killed, where did it occur, and when did it happen? As one reads through all the various statements, reports and biographies, one early learns that trying to put together a comprehensive timeline or location of events is simply baffling. When you read and reread the various statements, it seems akin to trying to find a blue needle in a blue haystack. It is very quickly apparent that many of the witnesses, as well as some of the early authors, not only had an inclination to one theory or another, but that many may well have had a personal interest in proving a particular theory.

This book will take the position that the seven Romanovs were alive during the daytime of July 16, 1918. From the discoveries that have been made of the common and secondary graves and the fact that there are no reputable reports of any of the seven Romanovs living substantially later, we will accept a date of January 31, 1919 as a point beyond which none of the seven Romanovs were alive.

One of the problems that has persisted over the years is that people distinguish between the two theories of either the basement murder room massacre of nine persons or an escape of some or all of the Romanovs. These two theories tend to be exclusive, since if there was a mass murder of all seven Romanovs in the basement room, then there is no acceptable theory of escape. Conversely, if there is an acceptable theory of escape, then not all seven Romanovs were killed in the basement room. People who accept the basement room theory seem to conclude that means that all seven Romanovs must have been killed in the basement room and their bodies loaded on the truck.

Let us examine something new. There is no reason not to assume that several people, including some of the Romanovs, may have been killed in the basement room, but there is also no reason not to assume that the Bolsheviks may have transported some of the remaining Romanovs alive or dead from the Ipatiev House, or dead at different times and not all at once. Certainly, while waiting to depart there would have been an expectation that all 11 persons plus their guards would need several vehicles for transportation. We will attempt to point out common sense answers to these alleged facts. We will take each of them separately and attempt to provide an insight into what occurred, since there never seems to have been a discussion of what would have been a logical conclusion to be drawn from the various scenarios.

The proponents of the theory that all the Romanovs left the Ipatiev House dead almost universally propose that they were killed in what is referred to as "the basement murder room." This was a room on the lower floor located between the larger outer hallway and a storage room immediately behind it. With all the investigation done in the house, one would assume that there would not be any disagreement about the physical facts of the room itself. Oddly enough, this is far from true. The persons who made the early investigation took measurements of the room, but for some reason their figures do not agree. Everyone seems to acknowledge that the east and west walls were longer in length than the north and south walls, making the room a rectangle. There was a window in the middle of the south wall and the entrance to the room was through two narrow double doors at the west corner of the west wall. There was also a set of wider double doors leading to the adjoining store room at the south corner of the east wall, the east wall being presumed to be the murder wall where the blood and bullet holes were found. There are also scale drawings which purport to be a blueprint of the room, but these show a more or less square room which is not found in any of the reports. In addition, the hall doors and the storage room doors are shown as very wide, with both of them in the middle of the wall, which is clearly not in agreement with the photographs. Unfortunately, the house has now been destroyed and numerous facts, which would be helpful, were lost in the demolition of the house.[20]

What evidence is there that this room was where the seven Romanovs and their four retainers were murdered on July 17, 1918? The first investigation was by Nicholas Sokolov, who published his findings in a French edition in 1924 and a Russian edition in 1925, which then became the accepted theory as a result of his findings in which he definitively stated that all seven Romanovs were murdered in the basement room. The main physical fact which supporters of the "Sokolov theory" believe buttresses that solution was that the east wall showed damage from a number of bullets, as well as bullets which were recovered from the east wall. At a minimum, this establishes that at least one shooter and possibly more stood in the room and fired revolvers aimed at the east wall. The other substantial piece of evidence was large amounts of blood staining the floor. Obviously, there were no DNA tests available at the time, so the best that can be concluded from this fact is that the blood was human blood. What do these two physical facts establish?

First, they could establish that people fired revolvers at the east wall with no one between them and the wall. It was established that the blood was human blood that stained the floor of the room. What can we definitely conclude from those two items? One thing we cannot do is to positively conclude that anyone was killed in the room. A possibility is that the shots were simply fired into the wall and that human blood obtained elsewhere was poured on the floor, all to establish a theory that this was, in fact, the murder room. There was no shortage of ammunition or human blood in Ekaterinburg in the summer of 1918. This theory is admittedly unlikely but included to show how little can be concluded with certainty from the wall and the blood.

The second possibility is that murders were committed in the room in the manner Sokolov describes with victims against the east wall and a firing squad on the west side of the room which resulted in death by shooting of the victims. The problem here is that there is nothing that indicates that the murdered victims were the Romanovs. It is equally as consistent with the evidence that the three male retainers, and possibly the maid, were the people shot in the basement room.

The wallpaper in the basement room also gives us another opportunity for analysis with respect to the size of the room itself. As mentioned herein, the Ipatiev House was described as a mansion. It was decorated and furnished expensively, so to describe it as a dank "basement" room is inaccurate. It was a tastefully decorated room. Obviously for persons who saw the room within several months after the murders, there was a terrible mystique that was felt upon entering the room. It was variously described as a "torture chamber" and as a room with "no exit." One can understand how these thoughts might arise, but quite simply there was nothing in the room itself that indicated it was a torture chamber, or that it was the room without an exit, in that it had a door which opened to the hallway, not unlike many other rooms in the building which had only one door as an entrance and exit. The owner was a wealthy mining engineer,[21] and persons who saw the residence say that it would have fit well in any of the wealthy neighborhoods in St. Petersburg. To illustrate the point, the different wallpaper in each room is illustrated in the following plates: Plate 1A is the daughters' bedroom; Plate 1B is the Commandant's office; Plate 1C is the hallway; Plate 1D is the master bedroom. That being the case, the statement that the only light in the room was from a single bulb hanging from the ceiling is probably incorrect. There are suggestions that the room was lit by a fixture on the north wall. There are very good photographs of the entire east wall. We do not know the measurements, but we do know the proportions. For those interested in a more detailed discussion of the measurements, see Appendix A.

PLATE 1A

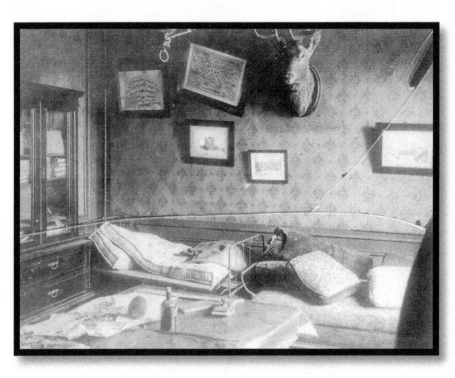

PLATE 1B

PLATE 1C

15

PLATE 1D

Yurovsky, who claimed to be the chief executioner, left a written description of the murders, which was discovered in 1989 in an archive by Edvard Radzinsky in the Central Archives of the October Revolution.[22] According to Yurovsky, there were 12 victims and 11 shooters in the room. Two of the victims, the Empress and the Heir, were seated in chairs with the other nine people standing behind them. Opposite from them were 11 shooters on the west side of the room formed in two ranks. The shooters all had pistols, meaning that all of them, including the front rank, were shooting at the victims with their firing arm extended. There is an attempt to say that some shooters shot through the hall doors into the room, but the doors to the hall were much narrower than the doors to the storeroom, and very few shooters could have fit in the door or the hall space behind it. Therefore, we get at least one group of shooters in the front rank with the muzzle of their weapons a very short distance from the victims. We will later discuss the claim that some of the victims had on an "armored vest" which consisted of precious jewels sewn in their clothing which kept the bullets from piercing their body. This applied to Olga, Tatiana, and Anastasia, but probably not to Alexei, and certainly not to any of the men. The maid is frequently described as having a pillow in which there was a small jewelry box, but she did not have any precious stones under her outer clothing. Given this situation and the firing of the more than 100 bullets (which would have required reloading by the shooters), it becomes very difficult to believe Yurovsky's account that very few of the victims were killed instantly and that it took some time to shoot or bayonet the remaining victims.

The aforementioned illustrates the problem that students of the Yurovsky Note have with the room size. From the two doors to the storeroom it is apparent that very few bullets went through the door compared to the space which was the wall north of the door. According to the above figures, we need to accommodate two people in chairs plus nine more people behind them in a wall and door area of 14'8". This is extremely crowded under any set of circumstances, particularly when you add the 11 shooters across from them. It is difficult to account for the reason the reports by people who measured the room seem to have in arriving at an exact figure. With three or four sets of measurements, they might be slightly different with respect to the width of the room, but one does not expect that they would be three or four feet different. Believing that, it appears the measurement of 8'4" for the wall area is very proportional to the size of the room.

The bullet holes in the wall area between the door edge and the pillars are hard to identify since large chunks of the wall were cut out in removing the bullets, but many writers suggest that the bullet holes in the lower part of the wall show the victims to have been kneeling. I do not believe that analysis is correct. As we will note later, I also do not believe that 11 people were killed in the basement room. My judgment is that at the start of the murders at least the three male retainers were shot in the basement room. I suggest the Tsar may not have been executed in the house, but if he was, there could be the possibility he was also killed in that room. The three servants, of course, were of no value at all to the Bolsheviks, and they were, in fact, a hindrance which needed to be removed. Further, I would suggest that the three of them died quickly in the early part of the murders. I also suggest that the reason there were bullet holes in the lower part of the wall was that the three men stood with their backs to the east wall and the scattered bullet pattern reflects the area between the three men and the area between the set of legs of each of the three men which would be hit by bullets, while the empty spaces represent the abdomen and chest of the victims in which the bullets lodged rather than lodging in the wall.

If that is correct, then we realize that this is one of many of the Yurovsky Note statements that become very difficult to believe. Everything about the size of the room and the bullet holes in the wall discourages the belief that 11 people were murdered in the room. We will remember the measurement problem when we begin to look at the other claims in Yurovsky's Note which also are a product of Yurovsky's contrived story of the events, and we must wonder why he had to create a contrived account of the events of that fateful night.

The Bolsheviks were not novices at executions. When they started to plan for the 11 murders, they basically had two options. One was to let the four shooters that Bykov tells us they used, shoot the victims in two or three different groups of perhaps three at a time. This would have been very easy to manage in the various rooms of the Ipatiev House. The other alternative was to let a mixed group of 11 shooters fire at 11 running, screaming victims in a small dark room. Common sense would seem to dictate that they would have chosen the former.

ALEXANDRA'S DIARY

When we attempt to reconstruct the events of July 16, 17, 18, and 19, we, of course, have no accounts available from the Romanovs themselves or attendants who were with them after the evening of July 16, except for the disputed purported account of the valet, Parfen Dominin, a non-existent person, and Alexandra's diary. When Yurovsky returned to Moscow after the events of that week in Ekaterinburg, he took with him numerous items of correspondence of the family, as well as written documents and their diaries. The diaries themselves are the last written accounts we have from the Romanovs for the period through July 16. Strangely, Nicholas's diary stops on the preceding Saturday, July 13, and it has no further entries after that date. Alexandra's contains an entry for July 16, presumably the last date they were in the Ipatiev House. The documents were found by the Bolsheviks, recovered from the Ipatiev House, and were hand carried to Moscow. Authorities announced that the documents, including the diary, would soon be made available. The actual release of the entire document did not occur and a translation was not available until 1997, at which time the last diary of Tsaritsa Alexandra was published by Yale University with an introduction by Robert K. Massie and edited by Vladimir A. Kozlov and Vladimir M. Khrustalëv.[23] The purpose of examining Alexandra's diary is because it is the only known non-Bolshevik source that fixed the family bedtime at 10:30 p.m. on July 16.

To understand Alexandra's diary it is necessary to read and reread the entries in order to get the flavor of her text. It is not a diary in the sense that we today would term a document a diary. It simply records a number of facts for each given day in a methodical, laconic fashion with no enthusiasm or disappointment. Alexandra habitually recorded each day's temperature and frequently more than one time in a given day. It is a book of the day's events in a very typical Victorian sense, which is understandable knowing that Alexandra was a Victorian's Victorian. The temperature is recorded for every day from January 19 through January 31, with the exception of the 21st and the 27th. In February it is recorded for every day from February 1 through February 10, with the exception of the 8th and 9th, and again on the 14th and 16th. On the 16th she notes, "-11° in the shade and -6° in the sun." On the 17th, she notes, "Sunned myself on the bench, -6° in the shade, -11°-14°." On the 20th she notes that it was -5° to -6° in the sun. These will continue but appear less frequently as the weather begins to turn warmer. For a further group of excerpts from the diary, please turn to Appendix B. This type of mundane repetition is typical of the entire diary. It will also include at the top of the page the name of the saint or church festival whose Holy Day it is, as well as an entry showing what practically every member of the European Royal Family has a birthday on that date. The balance of the entries deal with what portions of the Bible were read to her, the state of her health, and whether or not the others were allowed to go outside for exercise.

Not only does the last entry of July 2/16 have the short statement "to bed," but it also has the word "degrees" written out rather than using the small circle symbol for degrees which is on all the entries on all the days of the 6-1/2 months of 1918 covered in her diary. Why is that important? It is the only indication outside of the statements of the Bolsheviks that the family was in bed at 10:30 p.m. on July 16, which gives credence to Yurovsky's statement that he woke them up sometime after midnight. Nowhere else is there an indication that the family went to bed at 10:30 p.m. In fact, in Alexandra's entry it does not state that the family went to bed at 10:30 p.m., only that Alexandra did. Alexandra spent a good part of the day either in bed or reclining on a couch.[24] She was very inactive by the summer of 1918, so the fact that she may have moved to her bed at 10:30 p.m. does not necessarily signify that she went to sleep or that anyone else went to bed. The fact that there is an opportunity to alter the diary gives rise to the question as to whether or not anyone else might have added the last line of the last entry. Hopefully, a scholar will be interested in undertaking a detailed examination of the handwriting by an expert in order to provide an opinion regarding the authenticity of the handwriting.

What other evidence about the family's bedtime exists? In the letters sent by the Bolsheviks, which were purportedly from a loyal officer describing rescue attempts, someone, probably Olga, made notes on the letters.[25] In one letter the writer gives the number of rooms as three and puts their normal bedtime at 10:30 p.m. In script on the margins of the letter Olga has changed the number of rooms from three to four and the customary bedtime from 10:30 p.m. to 11:30 p.m. This is another instance where the generally accepted wisdom that the family had been asleep for over two hours when they were awakened is simply not a matter of fact and is very probably untrue.

TRUCK LOCATION

For a description of the removal of the bodies from the house and their loading on the truck to go to the burial site, we have to rely primarily on the evidence supplied by Yurovsky. As you read Yurovsky's Note, you may likely get the feeling that there is something rather strange about his narrative. He includes many insignificant details and sometimes without even a clear memory of those. It can leave the impression of a man telling a story that is not completely true while trying to augment it with numerous details. This is particularly important when we look at his description of the removal of the Romanovs' bodies from the Ipatiev House. Yurovsky goes to great lengths to detail the removal of the truck from the Bolshevik garage, with numerous explanations why it takes an inordinate amount of time for the truck to arrive at the house. He tells us that one of the purposes of the truck is to have it run with the exhaust at a high volume in order to drown out the noise of the shots. He says that the truck first parks in front of the house on the Voznesensky Prospect; later the truck goes west on the road on the north side of the house and backs into the courtyard gate adjoining the street. There are several problems with this location. Yurovsky says that the truck stopped at street level because the driver felt when the truck was loaded with bodies, it might not be able to drive up the incline from the basement door.

One substantial difficulty with this explanation is that when Yurovsky said the truck needed to be driven to the south end of the courtyard in order that the bodies may be loaded onto the truck, <u>there was no entrance or exit from the basement to the courtyard on the lower</u>

west side of the house. The basement had two exits, one being one of the two doors on the north side of the house and the other being the hallway exit on the south side of the house just west of the murder room. Yurovsky apparently forgets that at this point the palisade shuts off the south basement door from the courtyard on the west. The palisade started to the west of the basement door, went shortly south, then east, then north along the front of the house, and back to the house just south of the formal entrance. One guard described this as making a small courtyard on the east and south sides of the house. No one suggests that there was any exit in the palisade which would allow one to go from the south basement door to where the truck would stand at the bottom of the incline.

Why then does Yurovsky go into the whole amount of detail regarding the reason the truck wanted to go to the south end of the west side of the house to receive the bodies? If the bodies could not be carried there from the south basement door, how could bodies arrive at the truck location? There is one simple answer to that problem. This study suggests that some of the family were killed in the Tsar's bedroom on the southeast corner of the upper floor, or another upstairs room, and the bodies moved to the Tsar's bedroom.

For purposes of understanding the floor plan and use of the house, it is necessary to remember that this was more correctly described as a mansion than a house. As previously pointed out, an observer says that it could fit comfortably into the area of the expensive houses of St. Petersburg.[26] There were three rooms along the south side of the upper floor. The room farthest to the west was occupied by Anna Demidova, the Empress's maid, and did not connect with the rooms to the east. The second or middle of the three rooms was the bedroom of the four daughters. The room farthest to the east, which had windows on Voznesensky Prospect, was occupied by Nicholas, Alexandra, and Alexei. These last two rooms were not both bedrooms when the Ipatievs lived in the house. The bedroom occupied by Nicholas was the Ipatievs' master bedroom, but the adjoining Grand Duchess's bedroom was a sitting room for the master bedroom. The only exit from the master bedroom to the rest of the house was through a door in the west wall of the bedroom which led into the former sitting room occupied by the daughters in July 1918. This room had an exit in the north wall which allowed you to go into the adjoining room, which is an east-west room. There was one other additional important feature of this east-west room which is that the west wall had a door which opened out onto the second story terrace. The terrace had a set of stairs which led down to the south end of the west courtyard, or exactly where Yurovsky said they wanted the truck to park. The only reason for the truck to park at the south end of the courtyard was if the bodies were carried down the terrace staircase from the upper floor of the house to the courtyard. All the doors on the second floor were intact and working, except that the door from Nicholas's bedroom to the daughters' bedroom had been removed.

If it had been possible to take the bodies into the west courtyard that would mean that the death squad carried each body from the basement door, up the incline to the street level, where they were put in the back of the truck. All of that area is visible from the street and the house occupied by Father Storozhev and his family just north of the Ipatiev House and possibly the second story of the Popov House. The Popov House was located across the street south from the Ipatiev House and served as a residence for members of the guard. In addition to exhibiting the removal of the bodies, the noise of the truck would be clearly heard both adjoining houses. With respect to the noise drowning out the shots, this scenario has the truck at street level at the northwest corner of the house and the shots being fired in a room partially below ground level at the southeast corner of the house. The location of the truck for the loading of the bodies is important since it could indicate in which room of the house the murders occurred.

There were four entrances and exits from the Ipatiev House. The first was the large formal entry on the east side of the house facing the main street. This entrance seemed to have been rarely used as only a few had access to the house. Presumably, the guards left and entered by one of the side-by-side doors on the north side of the house, one of which led to the upstairs and the other to the downstairs.

This again is simply untrue. If it were true as stated before, that would mean that any servants coming from the basement area to the upper floor would have to walk outside in the middle of a Siberian winter to take items upstairs. Why then were there two doors close to each other on the north side of the house? The answer should be familiar to anyone who has seen the television series "Upstairs, Downstairs."

In the first quarter of the twentieth century, well-to-do families had a residence, which was always divided into two floors and known as the "upstairs and the downstairs." The servants who were the "downstairs people" did not go upstairs to the family floor, except on prescribed errands, or if they had been specifically summoned. In the Ipatiev House, this was accomplished by an inner stairway in the center of the house which allowed foot traffic from one floor to the other. The purpose of the two north side doors was to allow the downstairs' residents to go in one door and the upstairs' residents to go in the other door. On the blueprint of the house, there was a landing for using both doors, but there was a floor to ceiling partition between the two doors on the landing. Therefore, people going in and out the basement door could not enter into that door and then go east upstairs. The purpose of the west door into the basement is described by guard Michael Letemin in his statement where he refers to the door as the "servants' entrance." Michael Letemin[27] was a member of the guard who was arrested by the White Russians when they found Alexei's dog, Joy, in Letemin's yard.

A meaningful sidelight is that the Bolsheviks were curious why Yurovsky said when coming down the landing, Nicholas crossed himself at the landing where there was an image of a bear or a stuffed bear. It was not the bear that was important, but the landing and the door. An ancient Russian tradition said that when you left a house for the last time and did not plan to return that you made the sign of the cross as you exited through the door. Apparently, Nicholas felt when leaving the house, for whatever reason, he would not return.

There was also an outdoor exit from the basement hall on the south side of the house which, before the palisade was erected, gave entry into an open area and the street.

The people who were allowed in the house, other than the guards, were the following:

> (a) two novices from the convent who came every morning to deliver dairy products. They never saw the Romanovs and apparently had very little access to the interior of the house. Their main contact with the guards was the

guards' enjoyment in thoroughly searching them every morning;

(b) on June 2 and July 14, a priest, Father Storozhev, and his assistant, Deacon Bumirov, came to the house and performed an Orthodox ceremony for the Romanovs. Father Storozhev was an Orthodox priest stationed at the nearby cathedral but who lived with his family in the house across the street next to the Ipatiev House. Father Storozhev says that on June 2 when he and the deacon entered the house, they went through the first outer wooden enclosure and were admitted through a gate by a guard. They then went through a small inner gate which was locked and was apparently an entrance to the doors on the north side of the house. He says they went through a side door and then up a stairway where they came to the inner main door, which is presumably the formal entrance on the east side;[28]

(c) on either one or two occasions, several cleaning women were allowed to clean and scrub the interior of the house. They were under strict orders not to speak to the family and presumably would not use the formal front entrance;

(d) the only person allowed to repeatedly enter the interior of the house and the area where the family stayed was Alexei's doctor, Dr. Derevenko. We do not know what entrance the doctor would have used.

When the first three Romanovs arrived, a smaller inner palisade was built around the east part of the house starting at the middle of two windows south of the formal entrance. It went to the south edge of the house and then turned west 90 degrees to enclose the south entrance. The purpose of this fence was to prevent the family from being able to leave the premises through the south door, which was at the end of the basement hall. Some time later they constructed a much taller and longer fence which ran along the entire east side of the house and enclosed the north end to the courtyard and the south end to the courtyard fence. In order to enter into the formal entrance there was a small door in the outer fence on the east side attended by a sentry which allowed a person on foot to go through the outer fence. The suggestion that the truck might have been on the east side of the house was always discounted because the tallest, longest fence on the east side prevented any feasible path to carry the bodies from the house to the truck.

This misses a key fact. The outer fence had a gate on the north side and on the south side which allowed a vehicle to drive from Voznesensky Lane to Voznesensky Alley. This is shown on the drawing on Plate 2A which shows on the north and south fences an opening entitled "Bopota," which is the Russian word for gate. Professor Telberg's publication of the witness statements of Yakimov also confirms this fact.[29] In describing the outer palisade he says,

> "This second fence has two gates — one facing Vosnesensky Lane, the second opposite them, in the opposite side of the fence, close to the gate of the house. Both gates were shut from the inside of the fence. There was only the gate which was near to the door of the house at the time we began to perform guard duty. At that time the gates that faced Vosnesensky Lane did not exist. They were built when we were there, as it was found that automobiles had much difficulty in leaving through the fence entrance on account of a steep hill. That was the reason why the gates facing the Vosnesensky Lane were constructed. The motor vehicles entered through both gates but they left only through the gate facing the Vosnesensky Lane."

This, of course, would have allowed the removal of some of the bodies from the house through the formal entrance or from the north entrance described by Father Storozhev and then being loaded onto the truck with no chance for anyone outside the outer fence being able to observe what went on.

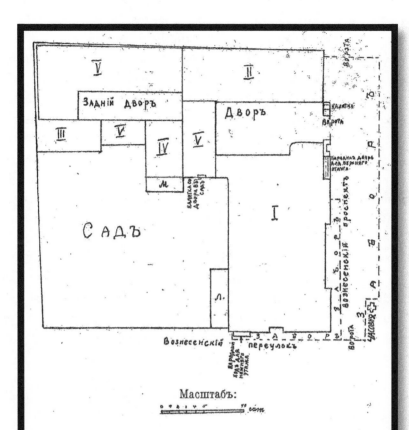

Масштабъ:

Планъ

усадебнаго мѣста Н. Н. Ипатьева въ г. Екатерин-
бургѣ съ указаніемъ построекъ.

Обозначенія:

I. Каменный двухъэтажный домъ.
Л. Терраса.
II. Каменныя двухъэтажныя службы.
III. Каменная одноэтажная баня и прачешная.
IV. Деревянныя службы съ каменнымъ погребомъ.
М. Досчатая бесѣдка.
V. Навѣсъ на деревянныхъ столбахъ.

PLATE 2A

29

Anna Anderson, who was the twentieth century's most famous imposter of the Grand Duchess Anastasia, fostering the legend that she had escaped, filed a lawsuit in Berlin in her attempt to prove she was the missing daughter.[30] The trial was very lengthy and was recessed during World War II. Years after the end of the war, the trial continued. In the trial in 1963 in Berlin, lawyers were able to locate a witness named Rudolph Lacher, who had been an Austrian prisoner of war living in the Ipatiev House in July 1918. He testified at the hearing, and his testimony was completely discounted because he said he had been locked in his room on the east side where he looked out a window and saw bodies wrapped in sheets being carried out the front entrance to the waiting truck. The testimony was discredited since everyone acknowledged that anyone looking out a window in a room on the east side of the house could not see the bodies being carried out from the basement into the courtyard on the north side of the house and then to the truck in the northwest corner of the house. However, if bodies were carried out wrapped in sheets, as he described, through the east front entrance and then loaded onto the truck standing inside the east outer palisade, as the study believes was the case, then Lacher had a clear view from the second floor window of any bodies being carried from the front entrance and then to the truck parked inside the palisade.

Later in life, Lacher made a statement that he served the Bolsheviks well and he kept his silence.[31] Obviously, the very thing he did not do was keep his silence as he described the murder victims being taken from the house. By keeping his silence he must have referred to something else that took place other than the accepted Sokolov story.

Besides Lacher, does anyone else say that the truck was at the main entrance between the palisades rather than back in the courtyard where Yurovsky places it? When the statements were taken from the Bolsheviks, some of the statements were questions posed by the local criminal investigating division concerning the murders. Many of the people questioned were not part of the murder squad or guards in the house but people who saw or heard something unusual at the Ipatiev House in the early morning hours of July 17. The importance again of their testimony is to indicate that Yurovsky's story of the truck at street level in the back courtyard is completely false and, therefore, bears on the creditability of his story of the basement room massacre.

A peasant named Buivid testified that he heard shots coming from the Ipatiev House.[32] He says that in about 20 minutes he heard "the gates of the fence open at the Ipatiev House and an automobile come out quietly into the street." All of the witnesses and parties use the terms automobile and truck interchangeably. P.F. Tsetsegov,[33] who was a night watchman on the Voznesensky Prospect, testified that about 3 a.m. he heard "the sound of an automobile behind the fence of the Ipatiev House." The guard Michael Letemin[34] states that he was told "the corpses were carried out to the yard through the servants' entrance and there to an automobile which was standing at the main entrance." The witness Anatoli Yakimov[35] says that after the murders "the murder victims were wrapped in these sheets and carried to the courtyard through the same rooms which they had been led to execution. From the courtyard they were carried to an automobile standing at the gate of the house in the space between the façade at the main entrance to the upper floor and the outer board enclosure. This is where automobiles customarily stood." Another witness, Paul Medvedyev,[36] states that Yurovsky ordered the detachment to wash off the blood stains and also "to wash the blood on the walls of the house at the main entrance in the courtyard and where the automobile had stood." He brought 12 to 15 men from the detachment who were first occupied "in carrying the corpses of the murder victims to an auto truck that had been brought up to the main entrance." All these witnesses relate that the truck carrying the bodies received the bodies at the main entrance on the east side of the house while parking between the outer palisade and the house.

Yet, a diagram of the house indicates large gates on the north and south side of the house in the palisade which allowed the truck to be placed exactly where these witnesses place it. Some confusion arises because on the north and south side of the house are streets that lead to the pond. One is called Voznesensky Lane and one is called Voznesensky Alley. The two seem to be frequently described by either name. A number of people put the street on the south side of the house as Voznesensky Alley while others designate it Voznesensky Lane. The diagram labels the street Voznesensky Pereylok. *Collins Gem Russian*

Dictionary[37] gives three Russian words for the English word lane. The last is Pereylok, which is described in parenthesis as "alley." Apparently the Russian word for alley can also be used for the English word lane.[38] If the truck was, in fact, standing at the main entrance of the house, this lends credence to the possibility that the bodies were carried from different rooms to the truck, and it also causes serious doubt regarding the accuracy of Yurovsky's description.

UPPER BEDROOM

We have previously discussed the fact that many students of the massacre have difficulty with the premise that 11 victims and 11 assassins were all in the basement murder room, where the assassins allegedly committed the mass murder. In the chapter where we discussed the dimensions of the room, it makes the scenario of the 22 people even more difficult to believe. The reason the basement room has gone down in history as the murder room is, of course, that Sokolov in his book positively identified that as the site of all 11 murders.

There are two things important to remember with evaluating Sokolov's book. The first is that he was employed by anti-Bolshevik White Russian General Dietrich who reported to Admiral Kolchak, both of whom were members of the White Army interested in showing that the Bolsheviks murdered all the family. The second is that the two previous investigators, first Alexander Nametkin and then Ivan Sergeyev, both began to have substantial doubts that all seven Romanovs were murdered in the Ipatiev House basement room. Both men were very quickly discharged. Sokolov, who was appointed by General Dietrich, understood that his job was to prove that the Bolsheviks murdered the family. For that, it would not be sufficient to prove that the family was missing and that there were bullet holes in a room with blood stains. But, Sokolov needed additional proof to show where, when, and how the murders occurred, as he had no bodies to offer for proof. No one questioned that some act of violence apparently took place in the basement murder room. Every person who examined the room found bullet holes in the wall, although the number of bullet

33

holes seemed to grow with the passage of time. Remember, there were numerous examples of blood stains on the walls and floor of the room, and Sokolov told us that scientific tests determined it to be human blood. At this point, Sokolov had a scene of violence and substantial amounts of human blood. This was a perfect solution for the theory that the Romanovs were murdered by the Bolsheviks in the Ipatiev House. It is still, however, an assumption, as there is nothing that indicates it was the Romanovs who were shot or that it was their blood staining the room. That leap of faith comes from Sokolov alone.

Sokolov had one crowning piece of evidence, which not only places the murders in the basement room, but identifies the Romanovs as the victims. This is the famous inscription in the German language which is a verse from the German poet Heinrich Heine. (For additional information about the possible origin of the writing, see Appendix C). The poem is based on a biblical recital in the Book of Daniel[39] which deals with a banquet being held by the Babylonian King Belshazzar. The Prophet Daniel interpreted the words which appeared on the wall of the banquet room as a judgment on Belshazzar and the end of his kingdom. That same night King Belshazzar was, in fact, killed by his own servants. The Heine poem is based on Belshazzar's assassination by his Jewish servants. The Heine inscription is written on the wall of a room rather than on a usual writing surface. The translation of the German inscription is as follows:

> "Belsatzar was on that same night.
> killed by his own servants."

Sokolov immediately interprets this as being written by the Bolsheviks bragging about their bloody execution of Nicholas II.

In the Romanov murders, the large percentage of leading Bolsheviks were Jewish, and the theme that the murders were Jewish revenge continually appears in the Romanov story. The inscription on the wall, which is handwritten, says that "On this night Belshazzar was murdered by his slaves," who were Jewish captives. The other additional Romanov tie-in is that the writer has changed the word "Belshazzar" to "Belsatzar", indicating that this was the room where the Tsar was murdered by his underlings. For Sokolov, this puts the whole story together. It not only proves there was a room where vicious murders were committed, which left human blood on the floor and walls, but the murderers then wrote an inscription on the wall of the room bragging that this is where they killed the Tsar.

The main problem with Sokolov's identification of the writing to prove the basement room was the Romanovs' murder room is where the inscription was first found by Judge Ivan Sergeyev. The second appointed investigator, Sergeyev was very methodical and careful about his investigation. In the winter of 1918, Sergeyev discussed the evidence with Herman Bernstein, a well-known American reporter writing for the *New York Times*. In his article which appeared in *The New York Times* for September 5, 1920, Bernstein is reviewing the book *RESCUING THE TSAR*.[40] This is a strange volume by James P. Smythe that alleges all the Romanovs escaped through Tibet and were living in Ceylon. Bernstein dismisses the book as an absolute fantasy. To bolster his opinion, he describes his meeting with Judge Sergeyev, who had a large folder containing the information he uncovered about the case. Sergeyev tells him that he does not believe the Tsar, his family, and the attendants were shot in the Ipatiev basement room, but he does think that the Tsar, Botkin, the maid, and the two servants were probably shot in the Ipatiev House. Bernstein feels that Sergeyev's account is basically true and that *RESCUING THE TSAR* is a fabrication.

Since Bernstein had been a Jew in Imperial Russia, he obviously has no kind feelings toward Nicholas. In his book *THE WILLY-NICKY CORRESPONDENCE*[41], he describes Nicholas as follows: The "Tsar is revealed as a compassionate weakling, a characterless, colorless, non-entity", and also as "feeble-minded."

Sergeyev tells Bernstein that he found the inscription in the Tsar's upper floor bedroom. Since it is Sergeyev who saw the poem when it was still on the wall and may have cut the inscription out of the bedroom wall, we have direct evidence the German inscription was not in the basement room. This study knows of no photograph and no one has ever indicated they knew of a photograph showing a rectangular space in the basement room wall from which the paper with the inscription had been cut out. From the photograph of the basement room, one does not see any empty space into which the wallpaper rectangle fits. No one else states that they found where the evidence came from or that they know of a cut out section of a wall from which the rectangle was taken.

One additional piece of evidence is an indication from the Omsk government regarding the location of the poem. In his book *CELEBRATED SPIES AND FAMOUS MYSTERIES OF THE GREAT WAR*[42] by George Barton, he tells us the following:

> "Late in August, 1919, the full text of the Omsk government's report, giving details of the alleged murder of the Tsar and members of his family, arrived in the United States. It was signed by Starijnkevitch, Minister of Justice of the Kolchak government at Omsk, and was addressed to the Director of Foreign Affairs. There is a repetition of many of the things already outlined in this narrative, and some new facts. For instance, it says that on the walls of the room in which the Tsar was confined in Ekaterinburg was the following inscription, made in German by an almost illiterate hand:
> 'This is the night on which the Tsar has been shot.'"

The room in which the Tsar was "confined" was, of course, the upstairs southeast bedroom. Therefore, the link which ties the physical evidence in the basement room to Nicholas II is false, and the only person who claims to have seen the inscription, when it was still on the wall, says that it was in the upstairs bedroom.

To examine Sokolov's work even more closely, the study obtained a copy of Sokolov's French text published in 1924 by Payot in Paris, where Sokolov had been living, and a copy of his Russian text published by Slowo in Berlin in 1925. Both were compared with John F. O'Conor's book *THE SOKOLOV INVESTIGATION*. O'Conor, who has not received his historical due, was the first writer to try and disassemble the Sokolov theory, pointing out the discrepancies in the Sokolov account. In his book, O'Conor includes the first English translation from the original Russian edition of the Sokolov report, which translation is done by O'Conor. A close examination will show that there has been substantial editing when comparing the Russian edition with the French edition. With respect to the point in question of the inscription in the basement murder room, the photograph (Plate 3A) omitted from the French edition was crucial.

PLATE 3A

Both editions show the inscription of the German poem. It is on a piece of light colored wallpaper (Plate 3B) which had obviously been removed from a wall. The paper itself has been examined many times. One of the more recent has been a Romanov exhibit in 2006 that contained the original cutout piece of wallpaper. Compare this wallpaper containing the poem with the decorative wallpaper in the basement murder room (Plate 3C), which is completely different. If you will examine the picture of the wallpaper on which the German poem is written, you will note that it does not have decorated columns. It has columns of four lines interspersed with plain columns. <u>Clearly the wallpaper on which the poem was written is not the wallpaper in the basement room</u>.

PLATE 3B

PLATE 3C

Was there any place in the house which apparently had paper that matched the inscription wallpaper? A photograph (Plate 3B) of the bedroom wallpaper of Nicholas, Alexei, and Alexandra on the second floor had paper which <u>matched</u> the paper bearing the poem. That in and of itself might not be convincing, but positive proof comes from the man who found the inscription. Recall that Inspector Sergeyev said in the interview with Herman Bernstein that he found the inscribed poem in the Tsar's upstairs bedroom.[43] Not only did the wallpaper in the upstairs bedroom match the wallpaper on which the poem was written, but the man who found it and presumably removed it from the wall said that it was not in the basement murder room. Note on the paper where someone outlined it in pencil before it was cut out. Sergeyev does not say whether or not he removed it, but if he did, there obviously was a matching hole in the wallpaper which showed the removal of the poem document.

The other alternative is that Sokolov removed the paper from the wall and then alleged that it was found in the basement room. Therefore, the entire Sokolov theory which rests on the Heine inscription is fatally flawed. Does that mean that no one was murdered by the Bolsheviks in the basement room? Of course not, but it does destroy the theory that we know the victims were all of the Romanovs because of the poem inscription.

Even more damaging, there appears in the Russian edition[44] a photograph of the poem (Plate 3B), as well as an accompanying photograph (Plates 3A). Plate 3A also shows pieces of wallpaper, and they are clearly identical to the wallpaper with the poem wallpaper. The description of the wallpaper in Plate 3A in Sokolov's Russian edition is identified as "pieces of wallpaper with spatters of blood." <u>Therefore, the wallpaper with the poem which Sergeyev says he found in the Tsar's bedroom is the same wallpaper he found in that bedroom which shows spatters of blood.</u> The conclusion is irresistible that although some people were killed in the basement room, other persons were killed in the upstairs southeast bedroom, and whoever knew about this situation also then inscribed on the wall of the bedroom the poem about the murder of the Tsar.

One item that might give a clue as to where the daughters were when the shooting took place is an examination of the bones removed from the mass grave. The bones in and of themselves present a mystery, as there are approximately half the number of bones that should be found in the grave for 11 people. Further, the bones are not in the form of a skeleton. They are jumbled and in many cases legs or arms are missing which may well be the result of post-mortem injuries. For this purpose, the critical item is the skull of the eldest daughter, Grand Duchess Olga. There is consistent agreement as to which skull is Olga's. There is nearly complete agreement as to which skull is Tatiana's. The major dispute centers on the skull of the two younger girls as to whether the body in the grave was Maria or Anastasia. With respect to Grand Duchess Olga, the central fact is that there was a bullet wound in the skull which by itself would have been fatal. It was fired from underneath the jaw and transpierced the skull upward with the exit wound appearing at the top of the skull just behind the forehead. An easy way to understand the effect of this evidence is to have a person stand next to you and place your finger in an upward position under the jaw and your finger from the other hand in a downward position at the top of the skull just back of the forehead and further right in the skull from the entrance wound. Clearly, this bullet was fired from below and transversed upwardly from the jaw through the skull. What can be learned from that wound? One, the possibility that Olga was standing up in the basement room when that shot hit is very small. The shooter would have had to have been lying or kneeling in front of her for the bullet to trace that path. The statements about Olga's death tell that she was killed in the first volley of shots and so quickly that she would not have had time to finish making the Sign of the Cross. If that is true, then the bullet wound we are discussing is extremely difficult to explain. One theory suggests that she was hit by bullets forceful enough to throw her body in the air, and while it was parallel to the floor someone shot through the skull. This study believes this suggestion is not credible. The other suggestion is that she was shot while lying on the floor. That physically fits the pattern since she and the bullet wound would both be parallel to the floor. The difficulty is that makes the shooter also be on the floor as the shooter, the bullet path, and Olga's body must all be parallel. In the case of her sister, Tatiana, no evidence is really available from her wound. It was an immediately fatal wound which transpierced the skull from the upper left cranium through the brain and exiting out the upper right area of the skull. Again, the majority of her bones are missing. This skull is not helpful from the evidentiary prospect, as the shot could have been administered while the victim was standing, sitting, kneeling, or lying on her right side.

Is there any theory that fits the wounds administered to these two older daughters? One suggestion is that they were shot while lying in a prone position. Tatiana's wound obviously could have been administered while she was in that position or a number of other positions. However, Olga's wound would seem to require a shooter who fires while she is in a prone position. The suggestion that Olga's wound was administered while she was standing behind her mother in the basement room is not credible.

DEATHS IN THE MURDER ROOM

Most observers are now willing to accept the fact that the bodies of the Tsar, his wife, and three of their daughters were, in fact, found in the mass grave. If one accepts this account that all five were apparently murdered, it does not answer the question of when and where they were murdered. Investigator Sokolov clearly puts the mass murder in the basement room, but other persons, including those who were there before Sokolov, are not nearly as convinced as he is. To a large degree he relies on three items: The appearance of the room, the Heine poem on the wall, and the statements of the Bolsheviks. As we have mentioned earlier, the condition of the room leaves no clue as to the fact that it was the Romanovs who were murdered there. Secondly, Judge Sergeyev, who found the poem, says he found it in the upstairs bedroom and not in the basement room; thirdly, everyone who examined the statements of the various Bolsheviks had considerable doubt regarding the entire truthfulness of any of the statements.

The report of the Tsar's death appears on the front page of *The New York Times* for July 20, 1918.[45] The *Times* headlining the article from London, July 20, recites the official Central Executive Committee message which, of course, deals only with the execution of the Tsar. There had been rumors since June 24 that Nicholas had been assassinated. The first of these stated that he had been killed at Ekaterinburg by Bolshevik guards. This report was denied by Russian officials, but this denial was closely followed by a Geneva dispatch saying that Nicholas had been executed by the Bolsheviks after a trial at Ekaterinburg. The last report was what purported to be an intercepted wireless message from M. Tchicherin, the Bolshevik Foreign Minister, in which it was stated that Nicholas was dead. Still another report was to the effect that he had been bayoneted by a guard while being taken to Perm. Obviously, on the day of the *Times* article there were numerous conflicting reports in circulation.

What was the opinion of the people who actually observed the room and had an independent evaluation? Questioning the scene was Judge Sergeyev, who was the second investigator entrusted with the legal investigation of the Romanov case. A review of the conversation the Judge had with a *New York Times* reporter, Herman Bernstein, appeared in an article in the *Times* by Herman Bernstein. Mr. Bernstein said he talked to the Judge in the winter of 1918 and asked the Judge whether he was really convinced the Tsar was dead. He said, "I am 90% sure that he is dead." The Judge went ahead to tell Mr. Bernstein what he had found, including, as we know, the fact that Judge Sergeyev stated that he found the Heine poem in the upstairs bedroom of the Tsar. He goes ahead to say, "It is my belief that the Empress, the Tsarevitch, and the Grand Duchess were not shot in that house. I believe, however, that the Tsar, Professor Botkin, two lackeys, and the maid were shot in the Ipatiev House."[46] The Judge also discovered the bodies, which was discussed earlier, of the murdered Imperial Romanov family members at Alapayevsk and examined them. He states that he had two groups of witnesses with respect to the murder of the Tsar's family, - one group stating that all were shot by workmen and Red guards, and the other group testifying that some members of the family were removed from the Ipatiev House alive. They talked of a mysterious German mission alleged to be sent to rescue the Romanovs. The Judge describes the second opinion as the weaker of the two. Mr. Bernstein concludes, "While there was a slight element of doubt in Judge Sergeyev's mind as to how Nicholas Romanov met his end, he said: 'Though we have not found the bodies of Nicholas and his family, we have found evidence that they have been murdered. The fact that the Grand Duchess Ella,[47] whose body we found in Alapayevsk, was murdered by the Red Guard leads to the conviction that Nicholas and his family met their deaths on the orders of the same people.'"[48]

Our next person who appears at the Ipatiev House in late September 1918 to conduct an investigation was Sir Charles Eliot. Sir Charles was not merely a diplomat, but was extremely erudite, educated at Balliol College, Oxford, where he took a double first in classic moderations and won several prestigious prizes. In his adult life, Eliot had a full knowledge of 16 languages and was conversant in 20 more. He had a very substantial stature in Russia in that he traveled in his own private train, which included a private dining car large enough to accommodate a table providing seating for 20 people. Sir Charles saw the evidence in the basement room and concluded that mystery surrounds the fate of the Tsar. Judge Sergeyev told Sir Charles that the statements of the soldiers were fabrications. Sir Charles's report stated that he examined the basement room and concludes, "There is no real evidence as to who or how many the victims there were, but it is supposed that there were five, namely the Tsar, Dr. Botkin, the Empress's maid, and two lackeys."[49] He recites a belief current in Ekaterinburg that some members of the Imperial family departed on a train on July 17. Sir Charles believed that it was possible that the Bolsheviks in panic killed the Tsar, but that it is the general opinion in Ekaterinburg that the other members of the family were not murdered. On the other hand, even though he thought that the Imperial family may have been disguised before their removal, the fate of the other Romanovs, as Sergeyev put it, "Cannot but inspire apprehension." The most that can be gleaned from Sir Charles's report is that on the date he visited the house, it did have bullet holes and blood stains in the basement room.

The children's French tutor, Pierre Gilliard, returned to Ekaterinburg to try and learn the fate of the Imperial family. In his book *THIRTEEN YEARS AT THE RUSSIAN COURT* [50] Gilliard indicates that he accepts the Sokolov theory of the murders. However, when he was examined by investigator Sokolov on March 5, 1919, he gives a very different impression. Fortunately, Professor George Telberg has preserved Gilliard's statements in its entirety in his book *THE LAST DAYS OF THE ROMANOVS*.[51] We find that the verbatim copy of the witness statements contain things that investigator Sokolov did not include in his report. Gilliard says, "At the time I left the house, I could not believe that the Imperial family had perished. It seemed to me that there was such a small number of bullet holes in the room I had inspected that everybody could not have been executed." Therefore, Gilliard is another person inspecting the "murder room" who does not believe the entire Imperial family was murdered there. His testimony is especially persuasive because he not only saw the room at an early date, but because of his close personal relationship with the family, he would have no reluctance in blaming the Bolsheviks for their murder.

The fourth of our investigators who saw the house and the basement room is Carl Ackerman. Mr. Ackerman spent substantial time in Siberia, also traveling with a number of people who had investigated or knew facts of the Romanov murders. To describe Mr. Ackerman as a journalist is not a fair description of his accomplishments. Ackerman, who was born in 1890 and died in 1970, was a correspondent during World War I with the United Press and later was a correspondent for other substantial newspapers. Ackerman became the first Dean of Columbia University School of Journalism and served there for nearly a quarter century. During this time Ackerman was a controversial figure speaking and writing with respect to Bolshevism and Fascism.

In 1919, Ackerman had published by Charles Scribner's Sons in New York a book titled *TRAILING THE BOLSHEVIKI: TWELVE THOUSAND MILES WITH THE ALLIES IN SIBERIA* (1919).[52] This book deals with Ackerman's lengthy experiences in Imperial and Soviet Russia. The main text of the book deals with political and economic matters, but obviously it contains reference to the Imperial family's final days.

Ackerman spent time in Ekaterinburg and spoke with Ipatiev, the owner of the house of confinement of the Romanovs. As is typical with every recount of these incidents, Ackerman gives facts which are contradicted by practically every other account. For example, he states that the four daughters slept on the floor in one room with scarcely any bedding. Everyone else places the four daughters in a bedroom with beds and bed clothing. He alleges the Tsar was frequently forbidden to see his wife, and they were seldom permitted to talk without a Bolshevik soldier present. He repeats the information that the family ate without sufficient plates and tableware and that soldiers helped themselves to the food while the family tried to eat. Again, this is contradicted by almost every account regarding the family's last days, including Nicholas's and Alexandra's diaries. He adds an interesting bit of information with respect to his inspection of the house itself. He tells us that the soldiers must have tried bayonet practice from time to time in the family's rooms. Ackerman says so many bayonet jabs were visible in the walls and ceilings of the rooms that apparently the guards in the house always had bayonets attached to their rifles. Descriptions of the murder room by most accounts gives substantial weight to the fact that the writer observed bayonet marks in the walls of the alleged murder room. Ackerman, as one of the few people to go through the entire house, tells us that that has very little evidential value inasmuch as the bayonet marks appear in rooms all over the house. He reports that the Moscow Wireless Station announced that the Tsar had been executed in Ekaterinburg, but the family was removed to a place of safety. Ackerman says that weighing the evidence regarding the Tsar himself, he should say that 6/10ths of the weight indicates that he is dead, 4/10ths that he may be alive. He offers by example many stories current at that time with regard to who was killed and when. With respect to the room, Ackerman says: "I saw the room in which they were supposed to have been killed en masse, but I was not convinced by the evidence presented there for these reasons." He does not believe there is sufficient evidence of blood and blood stains if 11 persons were killed. He also feels that the room was very small for the 11 person massacre and that there should be more blood stains in the other parts of the house. He further states, "I do not believe the evidence that the whole family was executed here is convincing. I think the Tsar may have been shot in this room, but on the other hand, there is the testimony of the Tsar's personal valet, Parfen Dominin, that the Tsar was taken away from the house early in the morning of July 16 by a small Soviet guard." Ackerman, of course, is the person who sent the Dominin statement to the newspaper in New York believing that he had the exclusive of a lifetime, so he attaches some credibility to the statement. His conclusion is: "Nicholas II, the former Tsar of all the Russias, and his family may be dead. They may still live. Who knows?"

The chief contribution that Ackerman makes is an amazing document which he alleges was written by one Parfen Dominin which relates in detail what happened in the house on the nights of July 15 and 16, 1918. According to this report, Nicholas was taken from the house and given a trial at which he was condemned to death and then returned to the house where he was allowed to bid farewell to his wife and son and then was taken away to be shot. Dominin states that Alexandra and Alexei were then taken away separately in a motor vehicle. The bizarre part of this account is there was no valet or member of the Imperial household named Parfen Dominin. There was a valet whose description met Dominin's in many respects, namely Terenty Chemodurov. Many accounts place Chemodurov in prison until the Whites liberated the city. However, this does not match the accounts of Chemodurov's departure in either Nicholas's[53] or Alexandra's diaries.[54] When the other members of the household are removed by the guards, such as Sednev and Nagorny, the diaries are quite explicit about the fact that they have been taken away, and in the case of the kitchen boy, Alexandra wonders if she shall ever see him again.[55] With respect to the valet leaving the house, Alexandra's diary for 11/24 May explains, "Chemodurov left as not feeling well – was completely undressed and searched before leaving the house." She gives no indication at all in that statement that he was taken to prison, but simply that he needed a rest. The statement of Parfen Dominin also contains an account of his being undressed by the guards at the house. Nicholas's diary for the same day is even more explicit. Nicholas says, "Decided to let my old Chemodurov have a rest and took on Trupp for a while in his place." (See Appendix D) We have an account by Alexei Volkov, who was the footman in the Imperial household, who went from Tobolsk to Ekaterinburg in the train with the rest of the household and suite. Volkov was immediately taken to prison on May 22 along with General Tatischev and Countess Hendrikova and Madam Schneider. As the White Army approached, the political prisoners were taken by convict trains to Perm. Volkov was imprisoned, and when on August 21 a guard came to the cell telling him to get dressed and follow the guard, he went to the office where Countess Hendrikova and Madam Schneider were waiting. The Countess had been a lady-in-waiting to the Empress and Madam Schneider was the Empress's reader. They had been held in prison with Volkov in Ekaterinburg and were transferred with him to

Perm. Volkov and the two ladies were taken on foot to a wooded area near Perm where Volkov realized they were to be executed. Volkov was able to make a break and race to a nearby wooded area and managed to escape. Meanwhile the two women were both executed at the site.

In later life, Volkov wrote a book relating his experiences in Ekaterinburg in the summer of 1918.[56] It is important because Volkov is able to tell who was with him in prison in Ekaterinburg and when. Volkov writes that after the children were taken from the train to the Ipatiev House on May 23, the next day, May 24, the valet Chemodurov was brought from the Ipatiev House and put in the cell with General Tatischev and Volkov. On the following day, May 25, Tatischev was taken from the cell by guards and never returned, presumably having been executed in the prison on that date. When Volkov was taken to Perm, apparently Chemodurov remained by himself in the cell. How does this relate to the Nicholas's and Alexandra's diaries? The best solution is that Nicholas thought he was giving his valet a vacation, not understanding that the Bolsheviks would not let the valet wander freely about the city, but treated him the same as they would do all the other members of the household and suite, namely those who remained in Ekaterinburg were either in the house, in prison, or under watch.

Ackerman spent what was a small fortune to telegraph this account to his newspaper in New York. He received the account from a nun at the monastery who had a written document from Dominin setting all of this forth in detail. Ackerman certainly gave it enough weight to send it to his paper, believing that it was the scoop of a lifetime. This is not submitted as proof of Dominin's existence, but to simply emphasize that none of the accounts coming out of Russia in 1918 or 1919 should be either accepted or dismissed without substantial study.

Ackerman and American Army officer, Major Homer Slaughter, (whom we will discuss later) had been traveling together through Siberia in Slaughter's personal railroad car. Major Slaughter received from Ackerman a copy of the statement by Dominin which Slaughter sent to Washington along with a note that indicated, in his opinion, this was the best explanation he had seen for the disappearance of the Imperial family.

The story of Dominin expands with the publication of a book *RESCUING THE TSAR*[57] published in 1920 and alleged to have been written by James P. Smythe. The central story of the book is that the Romanov family was smuggled out of the Ipatiev House through a basement tunnel and then taken on a wild journey which resulted in their arriving in Ceylon, where apparently they would live out their normal lives. The book is not universally accepted, but neither should it be ignored. The book does contain the only mention found anywhere to Dominin where we find the statement, "I must get rid of this old valet, Parafine Domino, who makes a nuisance of himself."[58]

There are a number of other entries in the book that need to be examined. Smythe says that upon meeting the Emperor, the Emperor will respond to a question with the code words, "Are you taking me to be shot?" In the Ackerman statement, when the Bolsheviks came to the Ipatiev House to take Nicholas for the last time, his question is, "Are you leading me to be shot?"

The book managed to spread in the West some doubt as to what happened to the Imperial family in the early morning hours of July 17, 1918.

RESCUING THE TSAR was published in San Francisco by a publisher who never met the purported author or knew the purpose of the book or what was to be done with it. The publisher is now known to be Henry Haskins. Mr. Haskins came to the United States from Russia in 1916 and started a small printing company in San Francisco. For the next few years, the company was reasonably successful and provided a living for Mr. Haskins and his family. A detailed recital of what took place between Mr. Haskins and the persons he dealt with regarding the book has been written by his daughter-in-law, Gretchen Haskins, with a forward by his son, David Haskins, M.D., in 1991. Her father-in-law's relationship with the author of *RESCUING THE TSAR* was beneficial enough to Mr. Haskins that the fees saved his printing company which was in financial trouble, and he went on to substantial business success in the printing field. Mrs. Haskins alleges that the purported author, James P. Smythe, is a fictional character. She says he was invented by William Rutledge McGarry, whom Mrs. Haskins identifies as the author of the book. Mr. McGarry had a varied background. He had come to San Francisco in 1917 to narrate the British war films. Mr. McGarry had numerous talents. McGarry joined forces with George Romanovsky, a sometime Russian consul to the United States living in San Francisco. There were numerous rumors circulated with respect to the fact that the Tsar might still be alive. Someone saw this as a great opportunity for a book. Having detailed information and names regarding 1918 Russia was not a problem as San Francisco had a very large Russian émigré population, many of whom were familiar with Russian court circles and the aristocracy. It was very easy for McGarry to gain information from these people. In addition, there were some publications available with respect to the murders. The previously cited episode about the "taking me to be shot" question is simply McGarry's borrowing from the Ackerman document, which was easily available to him. In the same way, McGarry "borrows" Parfen Dominin from Ackerman's story and puts him in his book. The questions that have lingered about the authenticity of Dominin because he appears in two different sources are easily settled by understanding that the second source simply copied the first source.

In her article, Mrs. Haskins indicates that McGarry "borrowed" liberally from other books. That is a charitable understatement. Mrs. Haskins is exactly correct when she indicates that much of *RESCUING* is liberally borrowed from a book *THE SECRETS OF THE GERMAN WAR OFFICE*[59] by Dr. Armgaard Karl Graves. Dr. Graves reveals that he was a former secret agent of the Imperial German government and was later to become an English secret agent. During his employment by the German government, Dr. Graves, like Charles Fox, goes on one secret, fantastic experience after another. When the German gunboat "Panther" sailed into Morocco and fomented a serious international incident, Dr. Graves tells us that Kaiser Wilhelm sent Graves with secret orders to the Captain of the "Panther," thereby preventing the start of a European war.

When you read Dr. Graves' book, you will find that Dr. Graves' experiences are very reminiscent of Charles Fox's experiences. Both meet mysterious persons and are involved with Imperial royalty, they use secret codes, they are able to manipulate people to their ends and move effortlessly through the most unimaginable incidents. To show how completely they are similar, here are examples:

Graves, page 99

"I called at the Nouvel Hotel Louvre where Von Wedel had told me I would find Countess Chechany . . .I was prepared to find a very handsome woman, but shades of Helen! This was Venus, Juno and Minerva - the whole Greek and any other goddesses rolled into one."

McGarry, page 28

"The titled performer of the Metropole looks like a twin sister of Marie Amelia, Countess of (CSZECHENY) Chechaney, a perfect composite of Juno and Venus and Hebe, all rolled into one."

The next example deals with the incident where each of them meets Kaiser Wilhelm II to receive a secret mission.

Graves, page 115

"Down a flight of stairs along a great corridor we made our way, no one speaking a word. At the end of the corridor we saw two sentries; then, a big solid oak door, guarded by an attendant in the livery of the Royal Household. At a sign from the Count, we halted. . .The door was opened by an officer of the Erste Guarrde du Corps. And, remembering our instructions, we entered and came to attention in the middle of a large room, facing an adjoining chamber, the portieres to which were divided. The room in which we stood was brilliantly lighted, but the other was dark, save for a green glow that came from a shaded reading lamp on a big writing desk. Sender looked at the desk and gave a sort of a gasp.

Then I quite understood his emotion. For seated behind that heavy, old-fashioned desk, was Wilhelm II, Emperor of Germany. . . I had seen the Emperor on many occasions but never so close before. . . Tanned, almost dark, his rather lean, face bore a striking likeness to Frederick the Great."

McGarry, page 29

"I was taken downstairs, along a wide corridor to a solid-oak door guarded by two sentries and an attendant in the Royal Livery. The door was opened by an officer of the Erste Garde; I entered a large room, advanced to the center, and faced the divided portieres of adjoining chamber! There sat the man whose nod shook the earth! Behind a heavy old-fashioned desk in a dim light, apparently absorbed in writing, sat a deeply tanned, lean faced, blue-gray-eyed counterpart of Frederick the Great."

In both books the parties involved share an amazing life event. In Graves on page 21, the author recites his terrible experience.

"On a rather rough, 4-foot, stone wall we halted, and the officer pulled out a document, began reading to me a rather lengthy preamble in Servian . . . and although it was quite obvious he was sparing for time, he seemed in no rush to execution . . . 'I can delay no longer'. He called a Sergeant, who placed me with my shoulder to the wall and offered me a handkerchief. I didn't want a handkerchief. A few sharp orders and 12 Mauser tubes pointed their ugly black snouts at me. . . .

How long we stood thus I don't know. The next thing I remember was a rattle of grounding arms and the sight of two other officers, excitingly gesticulating with the one in charge of the firing squad.

All three presently came toward me and one pulling out a flask of Cognac with a polite bow offered me a drink. I needed that; but didn't take it."

Clearly at the last minute the execution was halted and
Graves lived.

In *RESCUING THE TSAR* the narrator has the same
experience. On page 51, he tells us,

"and were conducted at the point of the bayonet to
the spot where I stood the officer of this firing squad
looked viciously at me and then ordered me to "fall
in." We were then marched to the log wall about fifty
paces to the left of the guard house and commanded
to "about face." When we did so we saw a firing squad
of 18 men in command of a Sergeant who gave the
order "prepare to fire!". . . He snapped and made
me about face to the firing squad for a few seconds
he held a silent conversation with the Sergeant that
functionary approached with a handkerchief. "Will you
be blindfolded?" he asked. "Thank you, I prefer to see
what's going on, I answered" . . . The squad raised their
rifles at the command of aim." I now know that he
felt positively nauseated at the moment, but he actually
SMILED "fire!" There was a rattle of musketry and
every prisoner beside me fell forward dead. I Stood
There Alone uninjured and alive."

Once again the two stories follow the same track with both
persons unbelievably being confronted with a firing squad, refusing a
handkerchief and then surviving.

The other completely unbelievable account in each book occurs in
Graves on page 135 "where he discusses a secret meeting at a hunting
lodge near the Black Forest. He is joined by Admiral vonTirpitz and
General vonHeeringen . . . At a quarter to 4 . . . the chug of a motor
announced the others, Lord Haldane and Winston Churchill . . ."

The purpose of the incredible meeting Graves tells us was that
England and Germany were discussing plans how they could join
forces and divide up France. Obviously, this is a meeting not reported

anywhere which no one seems to have ever heard of except Graves and McGarry. At page 33 McGarry tells us the following:

> "He was a great friend of Grey and Churchill at Monte Carlo and notwithstanding that meeting at Taunus they Must Be friends and Yet the Monte Carlo combination Holds good today. The Taunus meeting so far as Halden and Winston Spencer was a *frame-up* to Catch Waechter and "his whiskers." (both the Admiral and the General) that is where the Wilhelm Strasse Fell Down! and when on a mission of mercy, in behalf of one of the probable double-crossers."

It beggars the imagination that this impossible meeting between the German High Command and the first Lord of the Admiralty[60] and the Minister for War[61] for Britain is known to only two people in the world, Graves and McGarry, and appears nowhere except in their two books.

Anyone who believes that *RESCUING* is a true story of an agent named Charles James Fox is entitled to that opinion. Mrs. Haskins says that *RESCUING THE TSAR* is a fiction of McGarry's imagination and should not be used as proof or confirmation of matters dealing with the murder of the Romanovs.

The same is true of Graves' book. One reason these similarities seem not to have been noticed is that neither book has an index. Consequently, you can find the symmetries only by rereading both books completely. I think that for most readers, reading either one of them once is enough without suffering through trying to read and reread both of them several times.

Haskins' printing business had fallen off, and when he saw in the newspaper that the office of the Russian Consulate had moved around the corner from his office, he decided to see the consul with the thought that there might be printing work required by the consulate. Upon meeting Mr. Romanovsky, the relationship took a quick turn when Romanovsky asked Mr. Haskins if he could print a book. With very little financial choice, Mr. Haskins agreed, although he had no experience printing books. He was given a retainer and the manuscript and told of its great secrecy. Whereupon, he took it back to his printing business and began work.

There is no suggestion that Mr. Haskins was in any way involved in McGarry's mischief. Mr. Haskins was simply hired by a customer to do a printing job. If McGarry did not write the book for literary purpose or personal gain, why was it written? In the two year period from December 1918 to December 1920, numerus articles were appearing dealing with the Romanov murders. If you read the McGarry book, the Sokolov report, the Yurovsky Note, and the Ackerman-Slaughter reports, you would end in a state of complete confusion. It must be kept in mind that during that period there were numerous institutions and governments which wanted to circulate a particular story about the Romanovs for their own purposes. McGarry may have been instructed to do exactly that.

When Haskins finished printing the book, he presented it to Romanovsky, acting Russian consul. The book had an attractive cover but was filled with numerous typing errors and omissions and facts there were clearly incorrect. McGarry and Romanovsky believed the book had great possibilities, they felt that they could sell the film rights, and began to try to contact William Randolph Hearst to determine his interest, which turned out to be zero. Two things happened which were a serious blow to the book. The first is that Robert Wilton's book appeared on the market. Wilton's book *THE LAST DAYS OF THE ROMANOVS*,[62] although incorrect, had the ring of authenticity and came from an acknowledged professional journalist of good reputation who was on the scene. Wilton specifically states that all the family were murdered on July 17 and goes into substantial details about the incident, using the document written by his friend, the investigator, Nicholas Sokolov. At this point a second damaging incident with respect to sales of *RESCUING THE TSAR* occurs when Herman Bernstein, a New York journalist, writes an important review of the book for the *New York Times*.[63] Mr. Bernstein is scathing in his denunciation of the book as a fraud. He uses the "taking me to be shot" statement as having been copied from another book and was simply "plagiarism" by McGarry. The book also includes two purported notes written by Kaiser Wilhelm II and Nicholas II to Charles James Fox thanking him for his efforts in the rescue. Bernstein labels the documents "absurd." At this point sales lagged substantially for the book, and Romanovsky was unable to dispose of the 200 copies Haskins had printed. They were in Romanovsky's possession until he decided to turn over 100 copies to a store, the Emporium. This essentially constitutes the end of the *RESCUING THE TSAR* as the store was unable to sell the copies and they were apparently simply destroyed. There was no action by the United States government to halt publication or distribution of the book. It was simply did not sell.

In view of all the evidence that has been presented at this point, the question comes up, why was the conclusion of Sokolov so widely accepted for so many years? There are several reasons, one of which is that Sokolov was the first person to publish, which gave him an advantage as far as his version of the events. Sokolov explicitly finds that all the Romanovs and the four servants were murdered. With the passage of 10 or 20 years and no appearance by any of the parties, Sokolov's explanation became more reasonable and more widely accepted.

As already alluded to, the unfortunate aspect of Wilton's work is that people regarded it as an investigation separate from Sokolov which was done by Wilton himself, and, therefore, it added credence to the Sokolov conclusions, as Wilton comes to the same conclusions, which, of course, are simply his repetition of Sokolov's findings. He and Sokolov were close friends, and Wilton, in fact, was entrusted with a copy of Sokolov's report when Sokolov fled Russia in 1921. Wilton visited the Ipatiev House in the company of Sokolov, who explained step-by-step to Wilton the enactment of the tragedy. From his observation Wilton states, "We know from the deposition of the witnesses and the mute, gruesome language of the death-chamber where each of the victims sat or stood when the assassins fired their revolvers." Obviously, none of that could be concluded from looking at the alleged murder room. Wilton is convinced from an observation of the items found at the mine site that they proved the basement room murder theory, and he accepts at face value the idea that these items appeared at the mine site when the Romanov corpses had been transported there from the Ipatiev House and dismembered, burned, and buried.

Wilton describes the Romanovs' confinement in the Ipatiev House by saying that the Imperial guards, who were Russian, were brutal, but never attempted the fiendish ingenuity in tormenting their helpless captives that came to be displayed by the guards and executioners of the final week. He calls the Ipatiev House family meals "prison fare of the poorest kind" with stale black bread from the day before along with thin soup and meat of doubtful quality, with a tablecloth of greenest oil cloth and not enough knives or forks or plates to go around. He sets out as a fact that all the family ate with wooden spoons out of one common dish. There is nothing in the reports of the confinement, including the entries in the family diaries, which would support any of these allegations. In the introduction to Wilton's book, written by Mark Weber,[64] he praises Wilton's work; however, oddly enough he refers to a statement of Wilton's in which Wilton says, "The Germans approved the murders; there can be no doubt on this point." Weber, in his introduction, states that that claim by Wilton is not true. This is enough to give any reader caution with accepting Wilton's statements at face value.

Another illustration of Wilton's willingness to assert any allegation as a fact consists of his publishing a story that Anastasia took with her a King Charles spaniel, carrying it in her arms into the death room. Firstly, the King Charles spaniel did not belong to Anastasia, but to her sister, Tatiana. No description of the death scene mentions that a full grown spaniel was in the room with the victims. The thought that the members of the firing squad and the victims, all of whom totaled some 20 persons, did not notice a full grown dog racing around the room at the time of the slaughter is simply unbelievable. Wilton explains that by saying, "One pathetic incident escaped notice of all these witnesses." Wilton is then able to jump from that fable to the following conclusion: "Even in her death the little dog watched over them, and her mangled remains, still recognizable, brought final unmistakable proof of the end of the family."[65]

Wilton describes the murder room as 18 feet by 16 feet and identifies the firing squad with the names of five Bolsheviks and seven "Letts", the term "Letts" being a general description of men from the Baltic region. In describing the massacre, he follows statements which can be considered as true only if you believe the massacre occurred in the basement room and the murderers were honest in relating what took place. Wilton tells us that Alexei remained alive in spite of his wounds and that one of the girls, probably Anastasia, rolled about and screamed and that she fought desperately with one of the murderers, and the maid servant lived the longest. He believed that the murderers had not been able to aim straight at the boy and girl. He knew that the reason for that was that "even their callous hearts had wavered."

Wilton cites as proof of these details the evidence of three persons present at the scene, one being Paul Medvedev, who denied being a shooter but whose wife said that he was a shooter. His reliability has been questioned severely over the years. Medvedev, who would have been one of the most wanted men in Russia, purportedly surrendered to the White Army and died in custody. The second witness was a guard, Anatoly Yakimov. He did not witness any of the occurrence and stated that everything he knew was told to him by the sentries. The last witness is Philip Proskuriakov, also a guard. He, likewise, did not see the actual murder, having been locked up for being drunk, but claimed that he washed the blood off the floor and walls, although at the time he saw the murder room, any bodies had been taken out. Our three witnesses, therefore, are Medvedev, a man whose behavior would seem to be unbelievable, Yakimov who saw nothing, and Proskuriakov who saw no bodies. The last two witnesses establish at most that the basement room showed evidence of shooting and contained blood, but there is not one iota of evidence as to who the victims were or what happened to them or when.

Wilton never has any doubt but that the entire family was murdered in the basement room, transported to the mine site, and the bodies disposed of. Wilton, of course, does not have our knowledge that nine persons were buried in the common grave and that Alexei and a young daughter were buried separately. Interestingly enough, the Bolsheviks in September of 1919 brought to trial 28 persons arrested and accused of having murdered the Tsar and his family. There has never been any suggestion by anyone that this was anything but a mock trial in which the Bolsheviks tried to show that they had nothing to do with the Imperial murders. The point is that the Soviet's announcement states that they have "considered the case of the murder of the late Tsar Nicholas Romanov, his wife, the Princess of Hesse, and their daughters,

Olga, Maria, and Anastasia." The important thing about this statement is that the Bolsheviks in 1919 did not accuse their mock victims of also killing Alexei and one of the daughters which fits exactly the evidence uncovered at the grave site. Whoever prepared these documents understood Alexei and one daughter were not in the common grave and, therefore, were probably not killed in any murder room massacre, but were killed separately.

Wilton follows slavishly the story of the mine site occurrence by setting out what happened with respect to Yurovsky at the site. Numerous reports indicate that on the last day, the morning of July 16, 1918, Yurovsky ordered delivered to the house 50 eggs from the nuns who furnished food items every morning for the house. Wilton states that a year later they were able to find an egg shell at the site. From this Wilton is able to conclude as he explains that "Here on this stump Yurovsky had sat while his henchmen performed the last act in the tragedy."[66] Wilton is able to determine where Yurovsky sat and what he did by finding an egg shell a year later. This is pure fantasy. He also knows that the burial party began to hack the bodies in pieces at the pit site and that thereafter two pyres were lighted, the bodies cremated, and cinders thrown down the mine shaft. Again, this is not only a fanciful recreation, but discovery of the bodies shows all of this to be simply untrue.

Wilton reviews the evidence of the objects found at the mine site, citing the amazing fact that they find exactly the right number of corset stays to correspond to the six women victims, as well as military belt buckles that match Nicholas and Alexei's, which in his mind proves that those eight people must have been dismembered and their bodies destroyed at this site.

Wilton comments on the journalist Carl Ackerman's report, which also appears in this book, which Wilton determines is absolute twaddle. Anything that differs from Sokolov's report is immediately discredited by Wilton. Time and time again Wilton will refer to the murderous Jews and the individual Bolsheviks in terms such as "Yankel Yurovsky, the son of a Jew convict,"[67] and "Goloshchekin, the Jew Sadist".[68] The best proof of Wilton's prejudice is evidenced by the following paragraph in his book: "Sovietdom has consecrated three heroes to whom monuments have been erected: To Karl Marx, to Judas Iscariot, and to Leo Tolstoy, the three names that are associated with revolution, apostasy, and anarchism: Two of them Jews." Of course, no such set of monuments exists. Wilton's book is interesting as an account which sets out in detail one theory of the murders, but because of his complete adoption of Sokolov's theory and his violent anti-Semitism, Wilton's account is simply not to be trusted.

Shortly after the incident, Pavel M. Bykov, the Chairman of the *Ekaterinburg Soviet*, published a book entitled *THE LAST DAYS OF TSARDOM* in London by Martin Lawrence, Ltd. in the 1920s. His account contains no completely different facts in that he again puts the murder on July 17 in the Ipatiev House with the Romanovs' bodies being taken to the mine area in the forest. He is often cited for being the first person in the Bolshevik organization to announce the fact that the bodies were burned instead of being buried. This is a misreading of Bykov. Bykov simply says that the bodies were burned but there were remains and they were taken a considerable distance from the pit and buried in a swamp. He tells us that when the Whites retook Ekaterinburg, the persons who fell into their hands who were connected or knew of the Romanovs' death were executed, as were thousands of workers and peasants of the Urals. He specifically alleges that Pavel Medvedev was tortured to death by the Whites.

Prior to the publication of his book, he had written an article in 1921 entitled *"Worker Revolution in the Urals, Ekaterinburg, 1921."* This article, which was published in the West (in an abridged version published by Kerensky), Bykov makes several statements which are at odds with the standard story. He says that the original sentencing of Nicholas was done on the 16th and 17th of June, and was then approved by the Russian Central Executive Committee and Presidium of the Regional Soviet. On July 17 the Romanovs went to the downstairs room at about 10 o'clock in the evening and were forced to stand against a wall and were executed. Bykov says that the executioners consisted of only four men and that the bodies were taken to the forest where they were burned the next day. Interestingly, he claims the shots were not heard thanks to the noise of an automobile which stood next to the windows of the house during the time of the execution. This again dovetails with our allegations that the truck was parked next to the windows of the house itself and not in the courtyard incline. In his article, he reduces the story about the armored vest to saying that precious stones were found in the burned clothes which may have offered some sort of protection from injury. Bykov says that on the bodies of Alexandra and her daughters many valuables were found. "Gold and diamonds sewn into their clothes (in the bodices of the Romanov daughters in cloth buttons, etc.)." This confirms the maid Tegleva's account of the large jewels being sewn separately in cloth to make them into buttons.

More importantly, Bykov in the article confirms Beloborodov's statement with respect to who was in charge of the murders and the burial. Bykov tells us:

"Executing and destroying the bodies of the Romanovs was assigned to one of the most reliable revolutionaries, who had already participated in battles on the Dutovsky Front, and who was a worker in the Verkh-Isetskii Factory, Peter Zakharovich Ermakov."

But first, let us discuss the jewels owned by the Tsar's family more fully.

THE BULLETPROOF VEST OF JEWELS

One of the legends of the Romanov murders is the theory that the daughters in the basement murder room suffered an agonizing death because they weren't killed instantly in the first volley of fire. Yurovsky explains that the reason that happened is that each of the daughters was wearing a bulletproof vest comprised of precious jewels. The description requires believing that the daughters had on an armored type vestment in which loose precious jewels were sewn together horizontally and vertically so closely that a high velocity bullet from a few feet away could not have pierced the vest. It strains belief that a bullet fired from that distance would not have pierced the vest between two jewels either horizontally or vertically. This has often been referred to as the daughters having sewn jewels in their "corsets." No one has ever offered a demonstration showing how jewels in a corset could do what Yurovsky claims they did. Some of the difficulty may be caused by the fact that the translation of the Russian word "corslet" has been rendered in English as "corset", which is not a correct translation.

What do we know about jewels being sewn in the daughter's clothing? Our best account is that of the nurse maid Tegleva.[69] When Nicholas, Alexandra, and Maria went to Ekaterinburg from Tobolsk in April, the other three daughters and Alexei with servants remained in Tobolsk. Tegleva tells us that during that one month period of time before they left Tobolsk that all of them were engaged in sewing jewels in the daughters' garments. Her description is absolutely at odds with Yurovsky's account. Tegleva tells us that the jewels were wrapped in wadding and then sewn between two garments which the daughters

65

would wear under their blouse. From her description, the garments are more like brassieres than corsets. She describes the wrapping of the jewels and the two garments as being sewn together, leaving the impression that the jewels were surrounded with wadding and cloth. She also tells us that many large jewels were covered in wadding and then sewn into the garment as buttons or decorations on a hat. Everything she tells us leads to the conclusion that the jewels were wrapped in a cloth type padding, which would defeat the idea of a bulletproof vest.

There are a number of indications that the Bolsheviks in Ekaterinburg knew about the jewels in the clothing before the daughters' deaths. There are suggestions as to who might have told the Bolsheviks, but it is certainly more than reasonable out of the number of people who knew about the jewels and who understood by the middle of May the danger they were in, that one or more people told the Bolsheviks about the packed jewels. Further, while Alexandra was in Ekaterinburg, she, stumbling and bumbling as always, would send messages to the daughters at Tobolsk giving them instructions about "the medicine" or urging them to "arrange the medicine." Clearly Bolshevik censors saw these messages, and it would have taken a very stupid censor not to assume that the word "medicine" was a code word for something else.

If the above is correct, we need to know when the Bolsheviks discovered that the daughters were, in fact, wearing the jewels. Yurovsky's accounts vary slightly in that he says that the bullets that struck the daughters' outer clothing in some cases revealed jewels. He also tells us that the jewels were discovered when the daughters' bodies were undressed at the burial site. If this is true, we have bodies at the burial site covered in jewels which presumably the Bolsheviks scattered on the ground as they tore the daughters' clothes. There is very little detail in Yurovsky's Note about recovering the jewels other than vague descriptions that the torn clothing allowed handfuls of jewels to fall to the ground.

Who were the daughters wearing the jewels at the burial site? Yurovsky clearly states that they were Olga, Tatiana, and Anastasia. Why was Maria's body not also with the other daughters at the mine site? That is because Maria was not in Tobolsk when the jewels were sewn in the garments. Maria was with her parents at Ekaterinburg, and, therefore, had her clothes with her, and those clothes contained no jewels. Something very different must have taken place with Maria. This would be sheer speculation except that we now know that the mass grave contained the bodies of only three of the daughters and that the other daughter, now believed to be Maria, was buried in a separate grave some distance from the mass grave. The conclusion seems irresistible that the Bolsheviks knew which three daughters had the jewels and what they did with those three to recover the jewels.

One of the more impossible statements from Yurovsky is that when they were firing at the family in the murder room, the bullets that struck the daughters did not penetrate but ricocheted around the room like "hail." Strangely enough, in this small crowded room with 22 people, none of the murderers were struck by a ricocheting bullet. We have no explanation why a salvo of 100 bullets fired at 11 people with the bullets striking not all of them, but wildly ricocheting around the room, yet no members of the firing squad were struck, and the light fixture, said to be a bulb hanging from the ceiling in the center of the room, and the large window both remained undamaged.

This is our beginning as we show that whatever happened on July 17 in the Ipatiev House, it was not what Yurovsky describes.

MAJOR HOMER H. SLAUGHTER

This study does not investigate who ordered the murders or what conversations there were between Ekaterinburg and Moscow. Those items are covered completely in detail in many excellent books. It also does not deal with the authentication of the documents in general nor is there a detailed attempt to discuss and reconcile all of the many statements concerning the events of that night.

This study's two main purposes are to show that the Sokolov theory was either incompetent or, intentionally worse, biased from its inception and fatally untruthworthy. The second relates to the first, and that is that Yurovsky's Note and his oral testimony are unreliable as to the physical facts with respect to people, times, places and occurrences. If we do not accept Sokolov's murder theory and Yurovsky's murder room explanation, that does not mean that we can necessarily explain everything that did happen, but it does show that the accepted theory for nearly a century is simply incorrect.

We believe that we have shown that the truck that was to remove the bodies was parked on the east side of the house between the two palisades and not at the back courtyard gate. This fact is important because it not only discredits the statements of the participants, but also because it will help us place the room location in the Ipatiev House of some of the murders. We believe we have also shown beyond a reasonable doubt that an act of violence took place in the upstairs bedroom in the southeast corner of the house occupied by Nicholas, Alexandra, and Alexei. We set out that it is clear that the German poem referring to the death of the Tsar was written in that upstairs bedroom and not as

Sokolov sets out, in the basement "murder" room. That, accompanied with the fact that the matching wallpaper from the upstairs bedroom also showed splotches of blood, makes us conclude that either some of the Romanovs were shot in that room or possibly another upstairs room or that some people completely unknown for unknown reasons were executed there. Thus, the only reasonable explanation is that some of the Romanov murders took place upstairs. How can we conclude the victims were the Romanovs or their servants unless we can produce a witness who was in the house immediately after the murders took place?

Meet Major Homer H. Slaughter.

All the books published dealing with Ekaterinburg in July 1918 have shown us a number of people who played various roles. Many of these have not received the attention they deserve. It is often difficult to identify the various players in the Ekaterinburg scenario because in 1918 Russia, people frequently changed their names and identities, sometimes for good purposes and sometimes for reasons that are less honorable. An example is Sidney Reilly, who was known as the "Ace of Spies" and whose name at birth may have been Sigmund or Salomon Rosenblum or Rosenbaum or perhaps Lev Rosenblat. During the course of his life, he would have numerous other aliases; for example, Relinsky, Bergman, and Saloman Braunstein, along with many others. Ekaterinburg abounded with undercover agents, intelligence officers, double agents, and possibly triple agents. It was routine for foreign journalists to also serve in the pay of their particular government for the purpose of furnishing information. Two of the men present were U.S. Army intelligence officers whose role in the July events has not been sufficiently explored.

These two men who were both graduates of the U.S. Military Academy in the Class of 1908, had served together in the Philippines, and continued to receive posts together, including 1918 Russia. The men were Major Homer H. Slaughter and Major Emile V. Cutrer. Summers and Mangold first introduced us to Major Slaughter, and made several attempts to gain additional information about Major Slaughter. Unfortunately, their interviewees' information detailing his activities or documents was quite limited. Major Slaughter later appears in Shay McNeal's work[70] where she explains in more depth how Major

Slaughter was assigned in July 1918 to Ekaterinburg. She shows that the Major was not always where the paper trail would indicate him to be, but instead apparently he was involved in covert activities at a very high level. She also adds an extremely interesting letter which Major Slaughter's wife wrote to her mother-in-law telling her that Homer and another West Pointer were "going to stand-in for the Bolsheviks." The other officer referred to in her letter is almost certainly Major Cutrer. Although there are records that show Major Slaughter had left Ekaterinburg about the 13th of July, 1918, that is not the case as evidenced by a number of other documents. As an indication of the two Majors' status, they reported directly to their immediate supervisor, who was General William Graves. This in and of itself shows the importance of the assignments given to the two Majors.

A look at Major Slaughter's military personnel file describes an officer who was rated as very gifted, with a high degree of tact and ability in diplomacy. The ratings also indicate Major Slaughter seems to have been independently minded. He receives ratings as an excellent officer by his superiors. In 1914, Colonel Gordon's evaluation stated, "Has availed himself of his opportunities for improvement . . . should be entitled to important duties." The general estimate of his ratings officer states, "This officer has considerable ability, but is inclined to be argumentative at times; otherwise I consider him a very good officer." The Major's assignment records indicated that he was stationed in the Philippine Islands from April of 1917 until the summer of that year. About September 15, 1917, he was posted to Tientsin, China, where he remained until March 30, 1918, when he was detailed as an assistant military attaché in Jassy, Romania. The file indicates that he was posted to Vladivostok from March 31 to September 15, 1918, indicating he probably did not report to Jassy. He is also shown as the assistant military attaché to Russia and was given the temporary rank of Major and still unassigned to any organization. In September 1918, he is posted to headquarters Czech Army in Siberia, Ekaterinburg, and Tchelabinsk. He was again unassigned to any organization and his duty is given as attached to the Czech staff as liaison.

The report then carries a note in which Major Slaughter wrote that from May 19 to September 15, 1918, although the file shows his proper station as Vladivostok, he writes that during that time he was absent from Vladivostok and was actually in Siberia with the Czech Army for the entire period. His specific duties and whereabouts during late 1917 and 1918 are very vague. On his personnel report in December 1919 under the language section it says, "Speaks Russian badly." This would seem difficult to substantiate given his activity in Russia. Another efficiency report is dated June 30, 1922, at which time he was an instructor at the Military Academy at West Point. His rating officer rates him in Section H as superior on tact, initiative, intelligence, judgment, and leadership. Almost all his efficiency reports rated him as excellent or superior, with the exception that he sometimes is rated "satisfactory" in physical endurance and military bearing and neatness. His June 30, 1936, efficiency report describes him as outstanding and specifically that Slaughter "Speaks and reads Russian language." Now a Colonel in the 1930s, Slaughter also served as the commanding officer of the Far Eastern Section Military Intelligence Division with a superior rating.

In Homer Slaughter's file, there are typewritten documents and handwritten notes about his 1918 assignments. They read as follows: (See Appendix E for examples)

(1) To proceed without delay to Jassy, Romania, reporting upon arrival to American Military Attaché there for duty. February 16.

(2) Proceed from Jassy, Romania, to any point in Russia or Siberia where can get in personal communication with Lt. Col. Ruggles, Military Attaché to Russia. Report to him for duty as assistant. March 14.

(3) Directed to station Vladivostok, report by letter or telegram to American Military Attaché to Vologda, Russia. April 25.

(4) In addition to other duties, detailed as military observer with Armies in Russia. June 18.

No further handwritten notes appear until March 1919.

This study has also been able to obtain 120 pages of documents dealing with Major Slaughter's activities in Siberia from the National Archives. Starting with the pertinent parts, a War Department memorandum for the Chief of Staff states that the food situation at

Vologda was serious and asking that the food at Vladivostok consigned to Captain Wiggs be brought to Vologda. It says that Major Slaughter states that it is now necessary to go to Omsk and cities west to ascertain condition concerning movements of trains handling supplies. He requests an order by cable to take a railroad car loaded with food to the American Ambassador to make investigation and to return to Vladivostok. This train load of food occupies many pages of the file. This discussion of the train of food to Vologda is the subject of a telegram to the War Department from Slaughter on May 7, 1918, with the Milstaff Code. On May 19 Major Slaughter left with Colonel George A. Emerson of the American Railway Group, and a War Department telegram in code on May 20 directed to Major Slaughter tells him to proceed to Vologda with "car load of food."

The entire matter of Vologda requires explanation. The United States Embassy was in St. Petersburg, as were the embassies of all the Allied nations. The U.S. Ambassador was David R. Francis. Ambassador Francis was an 80 year old banker from St. Louis who had no previous ambassadorial experience and no knowledge of the internal Russian situation. However, Ambassador Francis did have substantial experience as the Mayor of St. Louis, the Governor of Missouri, and a member of the President's cabinet, as well as owning and operating his own business. Fortunately, Ambassador Francis also had a great deal of good common sense and his performance in Russia during this difficult period was as good as anyone's could have been and probably better. Ambassador Francis was the Dean of the Diplomatic Corps in St. Petersburg and functioned as the leader of the other Allied ambassadors.

The ambassadors decided at the end of February 1918 that it was prudent to leave St. Petersburg. Francis told the other ambassadors that he was going to Vologda, which as he explained was 350 miles farther away from the German Army. He indicated that if it became unsafe there, he would continue going east until, if necessary, he arrived in Vladivostok. He arrived with his staff in Vladivostok on February 28. The other ambassadors shortly joined him. The Bolsheviks insisted that he come to Moscow for safety, but Francis felt he was more likely to be taken as a hostage in Moscow than he was to receive security. The British agent, R.H.B. Lockhart (Lockhart was the personal representative from British Prime Minister Lloyd George to Lenin and a major player in Russian affairs in 1917 and 1918), who was inclined to rate Francis as of very limited ability,[71] stayed in Moscow and felt that Francis was making a mistake in not coming back. Because of Francis's judgment, he and the other Allied ambassadors remained free and eventually left Russia, while Lockhart remained in Moscow where the Bolsheviks arrested him and put him in the Lubianka Prison, where he narrowly escaped being shot. The Bolsheviks falsely alleged that Lockhart was the main conspirator in a plot to kill Lenin and Stalin.

In Ambassador Francis's memoirs of his time as Ambassador to Russia,[72] he describes his residence in Vologda. He was encouraged to stay by the local officials, all of whom called on him and were very courteous and accommodating. They offered him the use of an imposing structure for the American Embassy. He tells us that he gave a tea every Saturday afternoon for those officials, his colleagues, and their families. Francis said that the town was remarkably kind, and he enjoyed his stay there, and that he had entertained the local Commissar, the Mayor, the President of the Local Soviet, the President of the Duma, and five other officials at a dinner at the embassy. On July 4, he gave a reception for the diplomatic corps and felt that he was very comfortable there and never mentions any hardships or problems. This makes even more suspicious the trip that Slaughter discussed which would take a train load of food to the American Embassy at Vologda where, from the Ambassador's statements, it was not needed. There was a food shortage in Russia generally, but it does not appear to have been a serious problem in Vologda.

From May to August 1918, Major Slaughter's whereabouts become very difficult to determine. There are suggestions that at this time a train car load of gold bullion was supposed to be delivered to the American Ambassador. There is nothing actually in writing, but obviously the continual directions from the War Department in Washington indicate that perhaps the train of which Major Slaughter was in charge had something other than food on board. The Major told his family he had been in control of a railroad car of gold bullion.

We know that Major Slaughter was in the Ekaterinburg area in the middle of July 1918. On July 9, 1918, there is a telegram from

Colonel James A. Ruggles to the War Department stating, "Last news of Slaughter telegram dated June 19 received June 26 from Station Miass near Zlanoust." Ruggles states that the indication is that Slaughter may be on his way to Murmansk. Ruggles further states that Slaughter and Colonel Emerson and party then negotiated with Soviet authorities for permission to pass through the line. Later, a signed telegram from Perm seems to indicate permission granted and party now in route here. We know from Colonel Emerson's documents that he and Major Slaughter were both in the area of Omsk around the middle of July and that Major Slaughter did not leave with Colonel Emerson, who departed at that time.

There is nothing in the official file that deals with Major Slaughter's activities in Ekaterinburg during the week of July 14. Major Slaughter's lengthy report of September 16 to the Chief of Military Intelligence Bureau, General Staff, War College, Washington, D.C., states that the narrative section of the report will be found in the attached report of Colonel Emerson covering the period from May 19 to July 16, 1918. July 16, of course, is the date when Major Slaughter was somewhere in the area when Colonel Emerson departs.

At the end of Major Slaughter's single spaced, typewritten, 29 page report a sentence in script is added by Major Slaughter. The statement says, "A supplemental report covering certain details will be submitted as soon as practicable." It is hard to believe that the supplemental report, which cannot be found, does not deal with the Romanovs and July 16 and 17 in Ekaterinburg.

After this, Slaughter's whereabouts are so vague that it appears the War Department is not able to locate him. On August 21, the War Department telegrams the American Consul in Archangel, "Have you any news of Captain Slaughter?" On September 11, Ruggles telegrams the War Department from Archangel, "No news of Slaughter." At this same time on August 29. 1918, Major Slaughter's wife telegrams the army saying she has had no news of her husband in three months. The telegram states she last heard on June 8 that he was in Eastern Siberia. Again, the missing period of the summer of 1918. She requests information regarding his whereabouts. Attached to the telegram is a second sheet of paper in which the officer receiving the same forwards it to his superior officer to ask what Mrs. Slaughter should be told. The superior officer writes in script back to the first officer, "Tell her he is in Siberia."

What sort of man was Homer Slaughter and what were his duties in Russia in the summer of 1918 that seemed to allow him to go from place to place with no specific duty post and no specific orders? For a description of Homer Slaughter personally, we can do no better than read from his obituary in the West Point *Assembly* magazine for October 1955.[73] It states that during his service in the Philippines, he acquired from his fellow soldiers in the 14th Infantry Regiment "The bent that was to serve his country so well 1917-20 as the archetype of the WW II OSS officer, agent, and undercover diplomat, unsung in his feats of derring-do because of their import and potential . . . He was just outside of Ekaterinburg the night the Imperial family was murdered there and was the first outsider to visit the scene, investigate, and report." Major Slaughter's activity regarding gold is indicated by a photograph which shows the traveling "mint" that produced counterfeits of the gold secured Kerensky rubles and pictures Major Slaughter in the photo. Obviously, there was something not only special about the man but also about his mission. The family tradition is that the Major had the counterfeiting machinery in his private railroad car.

Major Slaughter was very circumspect and was not given to idle conversation about his service in Russia. What we do have are family oral traditions handed down from Major Slaughter to his three sons and their wives and from them to their children. If anyone would think that Major Slaughter embellished his pursuits or that his descendants have added to what they were told, you have no knowledge of Major Slaughter and his family. His brother, Stephen S. Slaughter, was the family historian and a well known author. He published a book entitled *HISTORY OF A MISSOURI FARM FAMILY.*[74] Stephen Slaughter was a substantial figure in his own right having done articles for *New Yorker* magazine and later became a photographer skilled enough that he was selected to take pictures for the Manhattan Project (the development of the first atomic bomb). Major Slaughter's eldest son was a West Point graduate and retired army colonel who after his retirement became a professor of medieval history. The second son was also a decorated army officer who served in the Battle of the Bulge and later wrote a published book about the battle itself and his participation. He was later assigned to highly secret duties with the army, including a station in Japan. The youngest of the three sons served in the U.S. Air Force. At the beginning of the computer era he was an acknowledged expert on computer operations and was sent by the air force to the University of California and to Harvard University. He subsequently worked for the Department of State and the Department of Defense being involved in setting up the computer operation for the Pentagon. He afterwards became the Director of Information for the United Nations and was in charge of their computer operation there. He was also a collector and expert on maps.

The qualities described in Major Slaughter and his sons were passed on to their wives and children. Any thought that these people would exaggerate Major Slaughter's services is utterly ridiculous. I have spoken to many members of the Slaughter family and would offer the family as an example of what can be accomplished by disciplined, hardworking, ethical people.

Having said that, what are the traditions that have been handed down in the family? The first is, as the West Point obituary states, he was in Ekaterinburg immediately after the death of the Imperial family. Further, that he was in the Ipatiev House shortly after the family was killed or removed and was allowed to go through the house with the permission of the Bolsheviks. As noted, his obituary said he visited the scene, and Major Slaughter always told his family that he was in the house immediately after the murders. The question of why that would be allowed has a very logical answer. It was at the time that the Allied armies, including the United States, were considering invading Russia with the purpose of defeating the Bolsheviks. The movement was not necessarily designed to restore the Imperial monarchy, but the Bolsheviks felt that was one of the possible goals of the Allied armies. The War Department files reveal a telegram dated July 10, 1918, sent by Colonel Ruggles to Murmansk using the Milstaff code. The telegram states, "Telegram received locally from officer of Whites Guard to effect 'things going on but we are anxious Allied assistance' . . . All Allied officials here believe intervention should come at earliest possible moment with largest Allied force practicable..." The telegram shows that it was also cabled to General Pershing at the same time. The reason for the Bolsheviks allowing Major Slaughter to enter the house was so he could inform his immediate supervisor, General William Graves, that there was no longer any reason for the Allies to invade Russia as the Tsar could not be restored, inasmuch as he was dead. As further proof, the family recalls Major Slaughter saying that he was then taken to the mine area of the forest where he saw the body of the dead Tsar. At the same time, Major Slaughter was shown a table in the house on the underside of which one of the children had carved the child's initials and a date. He was able to note the china on the dining room table which contained a residue on the plates of scrambled eggs.

By a twist of fate, the rural farm in Missouri where Major Slaughter grew up adjoined the John Truman farm where John's son, Harry Truman, who was roughly the same age as Major Slaughter, grew up and was well known to the Slaughter family. As a result, the Truman Library in Independence, Missouri, collected oral history from anyone who had information about the Truman family and young Harry Truman. Major Slaughter's brother, Stephen, gave a long oral statement to the library, which has been reduced to writing and is available.[75] Stephen Slaughter in his book first refers to the Ekaterinburg experience stating that Major Slaughter was "The first American and the first foreigner to enter Ekaterinburg the day after the murder of the Tsar and his family." He expands on this in his statement to the Truman Library where he says that his brother entered the Ipatiev House immediately after the removal of the Imperial family and the food from a meal was still on the table. The Major obviously saw the china still on the table and that may become an important point later in this story.

As an indication of Major Slaughter's importance during this period of time, an incident later occurred in 1919 when Major Slaughter was involved in a dispute with Ernest L. Harris, the Consul General in Siberia. Apparently, Major Slaughter advised the government that its conduct and policy in Russia were erroneous because they had been following the reports of Consul General Harris, which Major

Slaughter felt were erroneous in and of themselves. Obviously, this was not received well by Consul Harris. One assumes that such an incident involving a major would be handled at a local level with very little notoriety; however, Major Slaughter's transfer from General Graves to other duties in Russia under the direction of General Graves was accomplished by a personal letter from Robert Lansing, the Secretary of State, to Newton D. Baker, the Secretary of War. Secretary Lansing advises that Consul General Harris does not wish to consult with Major Slaughter and asks for the appointment of another officer as his liaison. In the file we find a personal reply from Newton Baker, the Secretary of War, to Secretary Lansing in which he advises that they will, of course, comply with the State Department's request and that he considered Major Slaughter a very valuable and excellent officer and there will be no problem of assigning him additional duties with the U.S. Army in Russia. Anyone familiar with the military will understand that the reassignment of an infantry major is not routinely a subject for personal correspondence between the Secretary of State and Secretary of War.

Having shown by circumstantial evidence, which is clear and reliable, that an act of violence took place in the upstairs room, the obvious question is, do we have any other factual evidence that would indicate that it was a murder and further that the victims were the Romanovs or their servants? For that proof we return again to our intelligence officer, Homer H. Slaughter, who as we have indicated was not simply an intelligence officer but what would now be referred to as an undercover CIA agent with the authority not only to observe but to actually take part, if necessary, in events in furtherance of his mission.

This study we believe has shown that the truck that was to remove the bodies was parked on the east side of the house between the two palisades and not at the back courtyard gate. This fact is important because it not only discredits the statements of the participants but also because it will help us place the location of some of the murders in the Ipatiev House. We believe we have also shown beyond a reasonable doubt that an act of violence took place in the upstairs bedroom in the southeast corner of the house occupied by Nicholas, Alexandra, and Alexei. We set out that it is clear that the German poem referring to the death of the Tsar was written in that upstairs bedroom and not as Sokolov sets out, in the basement "murder" room. That, accompanied with the fact that the matching wallpaper from the upstairs bedroom also shows splotches of blood, makes us conclude that some of the Romanovs were shot in that room. This study will reach a conclusion beyond a reasonable doubt of that fact based on newly discovered evidence from Major Slaughter's files.

In the *FILE ON THE TSAR*, Summers and Mangold tell us that they met with Major Slaughter's widow and oldest son and discussed the fact that the Slaughters had Major Slaughter's army trunk which contained his papers, and that over a period of time persons from Washington appeared and apparently took with them a number of papers which presumably dealt with the Romanovs' execution. The Major's eldest son, John E. Slaughter, Sr., who had possession of the materials, also indicated to them that there were lecture materials dealing with lectures that Major Slaughter gave after he returned from Russia to the United States. In one of those instances of sheer luck, we were able to discover additional lecture materials.

In the course of investigating the Romanovs' murders, I was consistently aided by my good friend and fellow author, Colonel French L. MacLean, United States Army (Ret), who added valuable insights and suggestions to the course of investigation. Colonel MacLean and I learned that there was a set of glass photographic negatives which Major Slaughter had kept in a wooden box. Colonel MacLean made a trip to personally inspect and photograph the negatives. These slides are not published, and this is the first publication to reveal that they exist and what they contain. One slide has a blueprint of the Ipatiev House. Blueprints of the house are numerous and are published many times in almost every standard work. When Colonel MacLean showed me the photograph of the blueprint of the house, I was surprised to see that it was the second story blueprint and not the basement blueprint, but at that time I was unable to understand why Major Slaughter had preserved a blueprint of the upper floor. I subsequently had the photographs enlarged, and over the period of several weeks kept studying all the photographs, including the blueprint of the second floor. On examining the blueprint one evening under a bright light, I found to my amazement why Major Slaughter had a blueprint of the second floor and not the basement floor. In the corner of the second floor bedroom of the Tsar there are drawn lightly in pencil three cigar shaped items which immediately strike the viewer as representing three bodies wrapped in sheets. (Plate 4A)

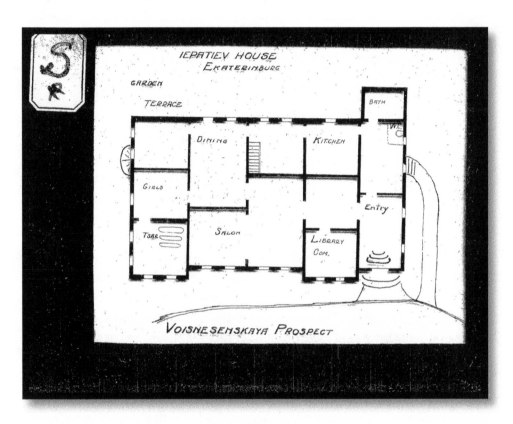

PLATE 4A

81

Given the scale of the drawing, these three items would appear to be between five feet and six feet in length. One of them is somewhat larger than the other two. There is no other conclusion other than they were drawn in by Major Slaughter as the set of slides has remained in their wooden container in Major Slaughter's possession until his death and in the continual possession of the family since his death. Until this discovery of the drawings, no one, including the family, was aware that the three figures had been penciled in on the blueprint and that they must represent what the Major saw in that upstairs bedroom when he was in the house on July 17.

Is there anything that suggested there were sheet wrapped bodies in the house? Yes, refer back to the earlier statement by Rudolph Lacher wherein he describes sheet wrapped bodies being carried out of the house to the truck parked on the east side. Further, the room in question was the Ipatiev master bedroom and the room on its west was the master bedroom dressing room. Those two rooms were connected by a door in the main bedroom west wall; there was no exit from the main bedroom other than into the dressing room, which became the bedroom of the four daughters. The only exit from their bedroom was in the north wall which led into the main dining salon. When the investigation of the house was made, a sheet was found in the dining salon on the second floor which contained blood stains made by someone who wiped bloody hands on the sheet. This had been a puzzle, as there seemed to be no reason someone would leave the murder room in the basement and come upstairs and wipe the blood off their hands in the dining salon and leave the bloody sheet in that room. If the three bodies in the main bedroom are sheet wrapped and another sheet is found with bloody marks in the next room, then a sensible explanation would be that the sheets were taken off the four cots used by the daughters in their bedroom and three of the sheets were used to wrap the victims and the fourth one was simply used by the murderers to clean the blood from themselves.

This leaves us with the main question as to who the victims were wrapped in the sheets in the main bedroom. There can obviously be a huge number of sets of three if you begin to arrange them from the 11 persons in the house. However, there are several sets of three that are excluded by a simple common sense evaluation. Certainly the chance that the three bodies are Nicholas, Alexandra, and the cook, or Alexandra, one daughter, and the valet makes no sense. They could be Dr. Botkin, Trupp, and Kharitnov, but circumstances make that very unlikely. Then there are the other main sensible sets of victims. One is that the bodies are Nicholas, Alexandra, and Alexei, whose bedroom it was. A second possibility is that they are Alexandra, Alexei, and Alexandra's maid, Anna Demidova. The third possibility is that they are three daughters. The suggestion that they are Nicholas, Alexandra, and Alexei is in conflict with a number of statements that Nicholas was shot alone in a military style execution. This appears numerous times, including the famous Parfen Dominin statement which, of course, contains several problems, but the lone execution was also the method of death which Major Slaughter told was his firm belief of what happened. A second important confirmation of the Tsar's separate murder comes from Prince Max of Baden. He was in a position as the son-in-law of Thyra, Duchess of Cumberland, who was a sister of the dowager Empress, to have whatever information the family might have received. In addition, his wife, Marie Louise, was the sister of Ernest Augustus, Duke of Brunswick, who married Viktoria Luise, the only daughter of Kaiser Wilhelm II in 1913, so his wife's brother was the Kaiser's son-in-law. Further, Prince Max served as the Chancellor of Germany in 1918, and as such was able to know all the information that was available to the German government, which was substantial. Prince Max stated that he had knowledge that the Tsar was shot separately at a military style execution. The forensic examination of the body of Nicholas II shows that he was struck by a number of bullets in the chest in a pattern that would fit a military style execution by a firing squad. This suggests that the three figures on the blueprint are either Alexandra, Demidova and probably Alexei, or that they are three of the four daughters.

If you refer back to the chapter on the levels of burial of victims, you will note that Alexandra and her maid were buried together in the top tier and that Alexei was buried in a separate grave. If Nicholas was, in fact, taken away and shot in a military style execution, certainly Demidova would have immediately been with the Empress and Alexei in the main bedroom. We are able to advance no other suggestion as to why the bodies were buried in three tiers in the grave, with the three tiers being segregated by gender and also by age, but the large probability is that the Empress and her maid were killed separately from the others, as was Alexei, and they were not part of any alleged mass murder in the basement room.

THE BODIES AND THE BURIALS

The discovery of the two gravesites has raised as many questions as it has answered. The first gravesite revealed to the public contained the bodies of nine people. This study takes the position that five of them were Nicholas, his wife, and three daughters. This is not dependent solely on the DNA results, but on the fact that according to the forensic examiners, the nine bodies meet correctly the physical description of the persons they are believed to be. American forensic examiner, Dr. William Maples, and his team gave gender, height and age estimates for the nine sets of remains. Their results are impressive, but they, of course, are not infallible. As an example, one of the comparisons they use are the photographs of the four daughters taken before the abdication. These show the daughters always in formal dress, and Anastasia was substantially shorter than the others. However, this is not solely because of her physical height. Anastasia had a deformity of the foot known as Hallux Valgus which causes the large toe to not be parallel to the other four but to cross over on the top of the toe next to it. This is a serious and painful condition and one of the courses of treatment in use at that time was that the person may only wear low heeled shoes. Since the other three are in formal dress and are old enough in those pictures, they doubtless wear high heeled shoes, so part of the difference between Anastasia and her three sisters is not body height but is created by the different height of the shoe heels. It is, of course, possible that the Bolsheviks selected nine other persons to match those victims, but I believe the weight of the physical evidence would agree with the results of the DNA testing. The suggestion that these are a second set of matching bodies becomes a more difficult theory if you look at other physical items in the remains. There is a rib which was broken during life and knitted back together during life which matches an experience of Nicholas. Certainly finding a broken rib would not be impossible, but again, it is another element that the Bolsheviks would have to have covered. Secondly, one of the skulls clearly shows that the person wore an upper plate of dentures during his lifetime. Again, this is not impossible to find, but the odds begin to go up at this point when this skull matches what you should find for Dr. Botkin. The last physical evidence, which is very substantial, concerns the fact that one skull held extensive dental work, including expensive crowns and platinum bridgework of a very high order. Finding a skull with that dental work might not be completely impossible, but it certainly limits the possibilities to a very, very small group of individuals. When these three things are considered together, they substantially weigh heavily that these are the bodies of the Romanovs. The second grave, which was revealed later, is somewhat close to the first mass grave and contains what are said to be the remains of two individuals, - a male victim in his early teens and a female victim in her late teens.

Let us first turn to the questions about the mass grave. One unfortunate situation occurred when diagrams were published showing the relative location of the remains of the nine victims. Unfortunately this drawing, while exactly correct as to location, leaves the impression that all the remains were on the same depth in the grave. Very importantly, this is not true. The results of the exhumation show that the bodies start as approximately 110 centimeters deep (47 inches). The remains found at that point, which were lying on the hard pan surface at the bottom of the grave, were Nicholas and the three male attendants. This raises the first question. The reports describe throwing all the bodies in the mass grave. Obviously, if the bodies on the bottom level were four males, the throwing of the bodies into the grave was not done haphazardly. Slightly above them were the remains of three daughters, and then above them, the remains of Anna Demidova, and at the top, the body determined to be that of the Empress. Her remains were found at a depth of approximately 85 centimeters. Seemingly, the bodies were thrown in the mass grave in three different groups, the first being the four men, the second the three daughters, and close by the maid and Empress. Drawings show a commonly published diagram of the bones in the grave. It is completely accurate and of great help in determining where the bones were. Unfortunately, it shows the bones as if one looked into the grave from ground level to the bottom of the grave in that the bones appeared to be all on one level plane. We have noted this is not the case. The bones in place in the grave indicate that all nine people were not thrown into the grave haphazardly with the bodies all lying on the same level. Is there any reason for that particular order, or are we to assume that the bodies were in their placement simply by mere chance? Clearly, it shows the bodies were not thrown in the grave at random. What possible reasons are there for the differences? The first is, as explained later, that it was very possible that Nicholas and the three male attendants were killed at the start of the murders. As in accordance with our theory that the four males were killed first, it raises the possibility that they may have been buried first separately. Is there any reason to assume there may have been different graves? Yurovsky's Note indicates the possibility of three graves, which exactly fits the way the bodies were separated by age and gender. In addition, we know that there was a second separate grave at some point which contained two sets of Romanov remains. As we explained in a different chapter, the three daughters may have met their death at a different time or even a different place from the four men, and this study believes that three persons met their death in the upstairs southeast bedroom. This again gives rise to the possibility that the bodies were originally buried in three separate graves and not in the location where they were finally discovered.

A later chapter illustrates the reasons why it is more reasonable than not that the bodies may not have been in the mass grave when Sokolov did his search. The bodies in the first mass grave were brutally mutilated with the face of the skulls all destroyed. There is no proof as to whether those injuries were ante-mortem or post-mortem, but it is reasonable that they may have all been post-mortem in an attempt to disguise the bodies. The more troubling aspect is that half of the number of bones (800 of 1600) that should be in the main grave were not there. If the bodies were all thrown in that grave on July 19, there should not be any missing bones, and the bodies should be in a more or less proper skeletal formation. The bodies are not in any recognizable skeletal formation, as the bones are mixed up and look as if remains were more or less shoveled into the grave rather than bodies being lain in the grave. Certainly the bodies may have been partially dismembered before the burial, but if that is the reason for the missing bones, the bones that are missing should be a complete arm and hand or a complete leg and foot. This is not at all the case. Some skeletons show missing bones of an arm but bones from the hand belonging to that arm are there. In another instance, the leg bones of a skeleton are missing but bones from the foot of that leg are present. The missing bones do not fit into any recognizable pattern or rational reason for their jumbled location.

The second grave contains even more problems. The first is that the remains purport to be what is left after the two cremations in the forest. No knowledgeable person now believes that you could burn two bodies to ash on an outdoor wood bonfire in a swampy location and leave no remains at all after 90 minutes of burning.

The Bolsheviks' account of the murders changes constantly over the years. In the mid- 1930s, the journalist Richard Halliburton has an interview with Peter Ermakov.[76] Ermakov is easily the least trustworthy of the witnesses. Ermakov tells Halliburton that he is dying of throat cancer and is giving what is presumably his last interview. This is a typical Ermakov lie since he was not dying of cancer at all and lived for many years after the interview. In the only recitation of these facts found anywhere, Ermakov attempts to solve the problem of the wood for the funeral pyre by telling Halliburton that before the murders he had taken several tins of gasoline out to one of the mines, along with two buckets of sulfuric acid and a truckload of firewood. This is the only account by anyone at the time Ermakov told the story where he says that a truckload of firewood was taken to the funeral pyre site. Yurovsky, who took charge of the fire, never mentions in his Note that there is a truckload of firewood that he uses for the bonfire. This is obviously simply an attempt by Ermakov to solve what may have become a frequent question.

What was found in the second grave are a few bones which show evidence of burning, an amount of approximately 40 small pieces of bone, a piece of dress fabric, and broken ceramic sulfuric acid containers. The problems with these items are substantial. First, if the bodies are burned to ash, there are larger bones in the grave that should not be there. These bones show evidence of fire, but clearly that is easily done by putting those bones in a small fire at any time. More baffling is the fact that there is a piece of dress material in the grave which certainly should not have survived a cremation. Even more troubling is the fact that there are the ceramic acid containers. The second grave is, in fact, two shallow pits with one body in each, while the first grave had nine bodies in a single deep pit. Clearly, if these bodies were burned and the only remains are the small bones in the grave, there is no need to have ceramic pots of acid at the burial site. If the bodies are to be cremated, there is no need to pour acid on them first. If at the end of the cremation there are bones on which they wish to pour acid, there is no need to carry the ceramic pots over to the burial place. The only purpose the acid could have with respect to the second grave is to someday indicate to an investigator that the two bodies were treated exactly the same way as the bodies in the mass grave. One is impelled to the conclusion that this gravesite creates an illusion that there are bones of two persons, one of whom was a female, and that they are Romanov remains because the unexplained ceramic containers lead one to believe that this grave is a match to the first grave in that these containers match the ones at the first grave and, therefore, these are two Romanov bodies. Thus, anyone finding the second grave is impelled to the conclusion that these bones belong to the two missing children since there are two burials and the ceramic containers which serve no purpose other than to tie the second grave to the mass grave. The second grave is, therefore, very, very suspicious, and there are substantial difficulties in assuming that it was created at the time Yurovsky says it was. Once again, we find a situation that makes Yurovsky's Note, whenever written, an effort to match it to the physical evidence and the statements of the witnesses.

YUROVSKY'S NOTE AND THE OTHER BOLSHEVIKS' EXPLANATION AND DETAILS OF THE MURDERS AND THE BURIALS

At this point you may correctly feel that the proof that some of the Romanovs were killed upstairs is more likely to be true than not. If that is the case, what does it do to the traditional story of the Romanov murders? The only thing that it presumably does to the story of the executions is to show that not all seven Romanovs were executed in the basement murder room in a mass murder. It no way suggests that the Romanovs were not executed on July 17 or 18, 1918. In fact, it bolsters that theory. After nearly a century has passed, there is no reasonable proof that any of the Romanovs escaped from Ekaterinburg to ultimate freedom. There possibly could have been some who avoided the immediate fate on the 17th or 18th and were moved while alive, but there is nothing that reliably suggests that there was an escape and that some of the family survived for years.

One of the reasons that there has been so much confusion about what took place in the forest area is that, unfortunately, many of the writers, most of whom were Western, started with the assumption that the Ekaterinburg Bolsheviks were basically uneducated, incompetent peasants. Any study of the events reveals that to be the opposite of the truth. Firstly, all these men had lived as active Bolsheviks and survived during the Tsarist era, no small accomplishment in itself. In addition, we know that a number of the leaders were intelligent men with some

90

education. Yurovsky was intelligent enough to have qualified as an assistant medic during the war rather then being cannon fodder in the front lines. He also was qualified to serve as a photographer's assistant. All of his actions with the family, although they could be said to have been duplicitous, showed organization and a plan for the operation of the house and the preservation of the Romanovs' possessions. Phillip Goloshchekin, Military Commissar of the Urals, was not only the designated go-between from Ekaterinburg to Moscow and back, but he was competent enough to be a close associate of Sverdlov, the number two man in Russia. In addition, there is no question about the qualifications of Voikov, who was a graduate of the University of Geneva in Switzerland.[77] It is generally accepted that Voikov was the author of the forged notes sent to the family to trap them into believing a rescue operation was underway and which did, in fact, elicit answers from them which the Bolsheviks used to prove the Romanovs' planned escape. These letters are very cleverly written, intelligent and expressed in fluent French.

The theory that the Bolsheviks were bumbling amateurs comes from Yurovsky's statement which details 48 hours spent in the burial area trying vainly to bury 11 bodies with a large compliment of able men available.

Writers have puzzled why the Bolsheviks were so interested in having a secret burial that they threatened peasants from the nearby fishing village of Koptyaki with death if they tried to observe what was going on. Further, the Bolsheviks closed the small road which led from the village to Ekaterinburg which the peasants used daily to go to market to try and sell their fish and garden produce. Everyone in the village knew that the road was closed from the morning of July 17 to the morning of July 19 (for schedule of the sunlight hours, see Appendix F), and everyone soon knew that on July 17 the Romanovs were removed from the Ipatiev House. It is not difficult to conclude that the secret thing that the Bolsheviks were doing in the forest area, which no one could know about, was to bury the bodies of the Imperial family. The question has always been, if they were so interested in doing this secretly, why have a production that alerted everyone for miles around? I would suggest that this could be one of the great red herrings of all time.

With cleverness that has never been accorded them, the Bolsheviks understood that the Whites would soon recapture Ekaterinburg and the surrounding area and their first order of business would be to try and find the Romanov bodies. Therefore, the Bolsheviks had to do something which would mislead the investigators to the extent that they would never find the bodies. The Bolsheviks did this by designating a large, but fictional, burial area and then burying the bodies in a different place.

Sokolov may have been biased and untrustworthy, but no one suggests that he was lazy or incompetent. A great amount of time and effort was spent investigating the area the Bolsheviks had designated. Finding the bodies would be the capstone of Sokolov's investigation. A large group of men plumbed every few square feet of the entire area, and Sokolov went to the expense of bringing in the hydraulic equipment to pump out the mines. Yurovsky has the problem of telling us the bodies were buried in July of 1918 in the middle of the road in a grave covered by railroad ties. A widely circulated photograph (Plate 5A) shows Ermakov standing by the railroad ties, which appear to be much as Yurovsky described them. This photograph is certainly taken at a later date, probably in the 1920s when Ermakov visited Ekaterinburg. Yurovsky explains that when Sokolov investigated the entire area looking for a fresh grave approximately 6 feet by 8 feet where the bodies could have been buried, he observed an area of flat wooden planks approximately 6 feet by 8 feet which the peasants would have told him were not there on July 16. Yurovsky says that it never occurred to Sokolov to lift up the planks and look under them. This is patently absurd. Any planks in place at the time of Sokolov's investigation would have at least been picked up by one or two of the Bolsheviks to look for freshly disturbed earth. The reason this did not occur was that the planks in the Ermakov photograph were not the planks that Sokolov saw in his investigation.

PLATE 5A

We again must turn to the Russian edition of Sokolov's book, and we find a photograph in that publication (Plate 5B), which shows the planks Sokolov saw in the meadow in the road. You should compare the length and character of the planks in the Sokolov photograph with the planks in the Ermakov photograph (Plate 5A), as well as the growth of timber in the background. The obvious conclusion is that the bodies and the Ermakov planks were not there when Sokolov conducted his investigation. The Bolshevik operation was beautifully concealed and carried out and let the Whites spend their time and energy investigating an area which had no burial site. At some point the bodies could have been transferred to what is now designated the mass grave. Yurovsky's statement obviously must conform to that situation and to Sokolov's book. The Yurovsky Note is a masterpiece of combining all three problems. It also explains why all of the statements contain so many differences. It is because the 11 person massacre in the basement room and subsequent activities in the meadow did not take place. Writers have pointed out dozens of inconsistencies in the statements, as well as in Yurovsky's later lectures. Obviously, there are many differences because everyone was trying to recall in detail an episode that never took place.

PLATE 5B

Yurovsky may have put some clues in his Note, one of which is that he tells us that if "something bad" occurred during the burial sequence, the bodies could have been put in three separate graves. If Yurovsky's description of the burial experience is not a recital of "something bad," I do not know what is. This may be a clue from Yurovsky to tell us what actually happened on that week in July. There are other statements in Yurovsky's Note that defy a logical explanation. For example, he says that 12 people were killed in the basement room. Everyone familiar with the situation knew that there were 11 people in the house and who they were. Yurovsky tells us that were was also a cook whom he believed was named Tikhomorov. That person did not exist, but there is a man by that name that everyone would have recognized as the public prosecutor of the Perm District. This may be Yurovsky's way of illustrating how meaningless the document was. Lastly, no one now believes that there was any possibility that they could have burned to ash two bodies on a wood bonfire in the clearing within the space of 90 minutes. Equally ridiculous is his assertion that they planned to burn the Empress and Alexei, but instead they burned the maid and Alexei. We now know that the maid and the Empress were buried together in the top level of the mass grave, and if there had been any cremation, it must have been of Alexei and his sister, presumably Maria. To make Yurovsky's account trustworthy, we must assume that the bodies, even battered and destroyed as they were, left him unable to distinguish between two middle aged women and a 19 year old girl. When did the burial of the two persons in the second grave occur? No one knows, but it is necessary for that to happen and for Yurovsky to put it in his Note in order to make everything match. Is there any reason why Yurovsky did not put 11 bodies in the grave? He tells us that the reason is in case the bodies were found, people would not be able to identify them as the Romanovs if there were only nine bodies. This is a theory that fails to convince anyone. There is one possible reason why there are only nine bodies buried together, and the reason is that Yurovsky may have been missing some Romanovs at that point. He cannot have burial graves with less than 11 bodies. Unless there were fewer murders in the plan for July 17 and 18, Yurovsky's life might be forfeit if Moscow found out that is the situation and it was Yurovsky's fault. Therefore, he devises his story that two bodies are missing and is able to explain the discrepancy by saying that the two bodies were completely cremated.

CLOSING ARGUMENT

If you now agree that there was not a mass murder of 11 persons in the basement room, how do we explain the findings of Sokolov and the statements made by Yurovsky?

With respect to Sokolov, the previous evidence about the German poem inscription indicates that Sokolov may not have been above substantially altering evidence to fit his theory. He was so strongly wedded to the idea that the Bolsheviks slaughtered everybody in a mass murder that he is basically unwilling to consider or even report anything that doesn't agree with his theory. The two things that allow him to tie the Romanovs to the bloody evidence in the room are the German poem and the famous telegram which says the entire family was also killed. The telegram read as follows: "Tell Sverdlov family suffered same fate as head. Officially family will die in evacuation." The statements about Sokolov's knowledge of the telegram in the French version and the Russian versions are inconsistent as to what Sokolov knows and when he knows it about the words "family" and "execution," which he claimed would probably be found in the telegram. In addition, the phrase "suffered the same fate" has been the subject of speculation as to who would have used that particular uncommon phrase. In Gilliard's book, he states that when he met Sokolov during the first few months of 1919, he could not believe that all the children had been killed. Sokolov tells Gilliard that "The children have <u>suffered the same fate</u> as their parents"[78] (emphasis added). This is also at a time when Sokolov claims he does not know what is in the telegram and that he learns the exact language only when the telegram is decoded for him in 1920, but he can guess the words "family" and "execution" are in the telegram and the phrase "suffered the same fate" is part of his vocabulary. No United States court would ever admit into evidence a document to prove the truth of its contents where the author is unknown and its origin can't be proven unquestionably. This may or may not be a plant and it may or may not be forged, but under no circumstances should it be considered material proof to the extent that Sokolov does. In addition to the physical facts of the telegram itself, which are covered in detail in many excellent articles, starting with Summers and Mangold,[79] it is not even clear that the text of the telegram means what Sokolov says it means. It is equally acceptable to understand that "entire family" means all the Romanovs under the control of the Oblast Soviet, including the Alapayevsk victims,[80] and that they have now "suffered same fate", that is, the Soviet has met and condemned them to death just as they did Nicholas. In describing Nicholas as "the head", it is equally reasonable to explain that by referring to him as "the head", the words can mean head of the entire Imperial Romanov family rather than using the term "father", which would certainly mean only his wife and children. As pointed out in the Preface, the three Konstantin princes murdered at Alapayevsk had a legitimate claim to the throne, which was probably as good as that of Nicholas's first cousin Grand Duke Dmitri's claim, and better than that of his other cousin, Grand Duke Kyril. I am not proposing definitely that that is what the telegram means, but it is an equally sensible reading of the contents as opposed to the meaning Sokolov gives to it in his version of the events. For Sokolov, the telegram not only shows that his basement room theory is correct, but for him it is another example of the perfidy of the Soviets who now send a message showing that they have been lying about the safety of the Empress and the children. (Appendix G)

Interestingly, this is another example of how the text changed from the French edition to the Russian edition. In the intervening time, someone apparently made "editing changes" to the text. Lieutenant Abaza, who was the expert who translated the telegram in the French edition, now disappears, and the translator becomes "An experienced person on the staff of the Supreme Commander in Chief . . . In Europe he succeeds in finding the one Russian individual who has always been known as a man of absolutely unique ability and experience in the field. He received the contents of the telegram on 25 August 1920. On 15 September of the same year, he had the decoded message from him . . . On 25 August 1920 the essence of the Bolshevik lie became entirely clear to me, 'We shot the Tsar, but not the family.' For themselves, not between themselves, they had to speak the truth. The truth could not be avoided, it had to accept, the word 'family.' This word was given to me with the others on 25 August 1920. A specialist-technician with colossal experience and outstanding abilities had brought to light the message of the mysterious telegram." In this explanation, Sokolov no longer has the miraculous knowledge that the words "family" and "execution" would appear in the telegram. A wholesale revision of the telegram explanation is in the Russian edition, and Sokolov's previous explanations become dramatically downscaled. Lastly, Sokolov says, "Its key, obviously, was the word 'Ekaterinburg,' which had 12 letters." The problem with this explanation is that the word Ekaterinburg does not appear in code in the telegram. All of the above make the entire telegram evidence of dubious credibility.

With respect to Yurovsky's Note and the lectures, they leave much to be desired with respect to adopting their contents wholeheartedly as the truth. Numerous writers have pointed out endless conflicts between Yurovsky's Note and his various recitals, some of which seem to be an attempt to make things fit a certain set of facts even though he has previously indicated differently. A good example is that he later adopts the idea that there was a King Charles spaniel in the murder room at the time that the 11 people were killed. This evolves from other people's stories about a Romanov pet into Yurovsky's claim that Anastasia carried her pet spaniel into the murder room and somehow it escaped unharmed and apparently unnoticed by everyone else in the firing squad. This explanation is replete with difficulties. Anastasia did not have a King Charles spaniel pet; she had a small dog which is shown in a photograph and appears to be a Pekinese. The King Charles spaniel, Jemmy, was actually given by Vyrubova to Tatiana. There were also two other dogs in the household, a bulldog referred to as Ortino or sometimes Ortipo, and Alexei's dog Joy. Yurovsky's attempt to put an unnoticed and uninjured dog in the murder room while the shooting was taking place is simply not true.

Even more unrealistic is his contention that he completely burned two bodies to ash on an open air pyre of wood in the forest. No reputable authority now accepts that statement as true. The general presumption is that the destruction of the flesh and fat by fire in that situation would require at least five hours and would still leave some blueish white pieces of bone. This theory is advanced by others, including Ermakov and Voikov, who both insist that the entire family was burned to ashes and the ashes were thrown into the wind and, therefore, nothing will ever be found of the family, which we now know to be untrue. These are the type of things that make Yurovsky's testimony unworthy of credit.

It is perhaps also time to re-evaluate Yurovsky himself. Although he was clearly a member of the murder conspiracy, he does not have the maniacal, homicidal personality of persons such as Ermakov. Yurovsky's past history consists of employment and a period of service as a medic in the Great War. Yurovsky attends to Alexei and his medical problems. Sokolov's analysis is that this is another example of a demonic Bolshevik who talks and treats the young boy kindly, knowing that he is ready to murder him. There is no suggestion that this was Yurovsky's behavior other than Sokolov's conclusion. It is equally sustainable that his conversations with Alexei were genuine. That does not mean he would not be a willing participant in an ordered coldblooded murder of the entire family, but it does shine a different light on one aspect of his character. Part of his character has been developed on the theory that he was sent to the Ipatiev House as the chief executioner to prepare for the murders. The telegrams confirming the appointment do not indicate that. They indicate that the previous commandant Avdeyev was relieved because he was unable to maintain discipline and also had a severe alcohol problem. The guards were becoming lax and friendly with the prisoners, and Avdeyev seemed unable to control the situation. In addition, his assistant Alexander Moshkin was clearly guilty of stealing from the Imperial family and was also disciplined and dismissed. The telegrams indicated that the new persons coming on would restore discipline and that was stated to be the purpose of their assignment. Bykov and Beloborodov both indicate that the carrying out of the murders was given to Ermakov as a veteran revolutionary. Further, the Bolsheviks had been making preparation long before Yurovsky took over. They undertook a slow, but consistent, removal of men in the Romanov household in Ekaterinburg who might present a problem if there was a physical defense of the Romanovs. When the first Romanov group arrived at the Ipatiev House in April 1918, the Tsar's aide General Elias Tatishchev, who was aged 59, and the footman Aleksei Volkov, also aged 59, were taken directly from the train to prison. The next day Nicholas's valet Chemorodov, aged 69, was also taken to prison. Volkov indicates that the next day General Tatishchev was executed.[81] The two tutors, Sydney Gibbs, aged 42, and Pierre Gilliard, aged 39, were not allowed into the house. The Bolsheviks then removed Prince Dolgoruky, aged 50, who was living in the Ipatiev House and who was taken to the Ekaterinburg prison where he was shortly thereafter executed. The two youngest most physically fit of the household were Klement Nagorny, aged 29, and Ivan Sednev, aged 32, both of whom had been in active military service. They were both removed together and taken to the prison where both were executed. Therefore, by the week of July 14, the only men left in the house to attempt to defend the Imperial family were Dr. Eugene Botkin, Ivan Kharitonov, the cook, and Trupp, the valet. Dr. Eugene Botkin was 53 years old, overweight and in poor physical shape and would not have represented a threat to several 20 year old guards. Trupp, the valet, was over six feet tall and a good physical specimen for his age, but he was 62. The one young active man remaining in the household was Ivan Kharitonov, aged 48, who was the cook. It would seem to have caused a substantial amount of chaos to the living arrangements of the Romanovs if their cook had been taken away earlier. The three men left in the house were the only men present (other than Nicholas himself) to provide protection for the family, but in reality were simply no protection at all.

A starting point in determining Yurovsky's actions is to determine exactly what Yurovsky's function was with respect to the murders. The statements of Ermakov are directly opposed to Yurovsky's. Yurovsky tells us that he was the person who went to the family's rooms, woke Botkin, directed the family to go downstairs, supervised their placement in the basement room, brought in the firing squad, and read a paper to Nicholas informing him that they were to be shot. Ermakov's statement tells that he, Ermakov, was the person who went upstairs, awakened the family, and proceeded to take charge of the executions.

What independent evidence is there as to which story is correct? The first piece of evidence is the statement of Beloborodov, the head of the Ural Oblast Soviet, in which he states that he had Ermakov come to the Hotel Amerika, which was the Cheka Headquarters, to tell him that he had been delegated to execute the family and to bury them so that the bodies cannot be found. He tells Ermakov that that honor is given to him because he was an old revolutionary. Ermakov was indeed an old revolutionary and was the most honored of the Tsar's victims in that he had done time at hard labor as a political prisoner. Further, Ermakov's reputation was as a brutal and bloody revolutionary, having killed one man by beheading him. No one doubted but that Ermakov would be completely willing and even eager to oversee the executions. Since there are so many conflicting statements, Beloborodov's in and of itself is not sufficient to put Ermakov in charge of the executions. However, it is not the only evidence that Ermakov was early on designated as the person in charge of the executions.

We have referred earlier to Pavel Bykov, who at the time of the executions was the head of the Ekaterinburg Soviet. We refer again to his 1921 article in which he tells us that the executing and destroying of the bodies of the Romanovs was assigned to one of the most reliable revolutionaries who had already participated in the Battle on the Dutovsky Front and who was a worker in the Verkh-Isetskii Factory, namely, Peter Zakharovich Ermakov. Bykov goes on to state that when the Romanovs were assembled for the execution, it was the commandant of the house, who was also the head of the Ural Soviet, who read the death sentence. He tells us that during the executions there were only four men present. Obviously, it is important to square Yurovsky's statement, Ermakov's statement, and Bykov's and Belaborodov's statements with each other. Why would these four men, who were so deeply involved in the murders, have conflicting descriptions of the execution? I believe that the reason that these four men cannot agree on what happened and why the statements of numerous other Bolsheviks conflict with these four and with each other is the fact that the story of the 11 victims in the basement room is a complete fabrication, which obviously causes the statements of the Bolsheviks to have conflicts with respect to happenings that never occurred.

Yurovsky attempts to correct any indication that he was not unsympathetic enough where the Imperial family was concerned by saying that when the bleeding Alexei lay dying on the floor, he gave Alexei a hard kick with his heavy boot to Alexei's head in order to inflict additional pain on the dying boy.

A significant fact is that no one disputes that it was Yurovsky who proposed and effectuated the transfer of the kitchen boy, Leonid Sednev, within 24 hours before the murders, thus sparing his life. No reason is given why he should have been spared. He is believed to be about 13 or 14 years old, so his age was not a factor in that the Bolsheviks had no problem killing the 13 year old Alexei and the 17 year old Anastasia. In addition, he was a full time servant of the Imperial family and a playmate of Alexei, circumstances which would seem to be more than enough for him to have a death sentence. Further, the Sednev family was strongly monarchist and his uncle, Ivan Sednev, was a servant in the Ipatiev House, who was earlier executed by the Bolsheviks for his monarchist leanings. This would be another strike against preserving the life of the kitchen boy. You can be left with the proposition that taking Sednev out of the house was simply a humane act by Yurovsky. This book is not a rehabilitation of Yurovsky. He without hesitation joined in the murders and participated in every part of the gruesome undertaking. It is simply an effort to try and set forth all the facts which might be helpful in determining what took place.

When we investigate the murders, we have only the Bolsheviks themselves to tell us what happened. There would seem to be four persons who certainly were at the Ipatiev House that night and who would have knowledge of what took place. Those four persons are Yakov Yurovsky, his assistant Grigory Nikulin, Peter Ermakov and Sergei Lyukhanov. The first three were persons of authority. After the act, Yurovsky was said to be the chief executioner. He certainly was accompanied by his assistant Nikulin, who was so close to Yurovsky that Yurovsky considered him his foster son. The third person, Ermakov, is said by everyone to have been a participant in the murders, and Ermakov proudly claims that himself. The fourth person is in a different category. Sergei Lyukhanov was the driver of the truck that went from the house to the forest. He had a menial position but was a participant who knew everything that happened with respect to the removal and transportation of the Romanovs' bodies. We would assume that these four people would have accounts of the murders that would dovetail together. Nothing could be further from the actual situation. As noted before, Yurovsky said it was he who went upstairs in the early morning hours to awaken the Romanovs and tell them to get dressed, but Ermakov says it was he who went upstairs for that purpose. In addition, Michael Medvedyev says that he was the person directed to go upstairs and wake up the Romanovs. One conclusion is that there was no entire group assembly of all the Romanovs in the early morning hours of July 17.

What was the fate of these four persons after Ekaterinburg? Nikulin fared the best, being in a substantial position in the government at Moscow. Ermakov also did well and was regarded as a hero of the revolution. Yurovsky, who would seem to be the more important person, finally settled in Ekaterinburg where he was basically shunned by the residents.[82] We need to consider what the relationship between Yurovsky and Stalin was, as the Bolsheviks in Ekaterinburg had a troubled future with Stalin. Three of the leaders who were the persons who received Nicholas, Alexandra, and Maria in April 1918 when they arrived in Ekaterinburg were Alekasander Beloborodov, Boris Didkovsky, and Phillip Goloshchekin. All three of these perished in the Stalin purges in the 1930s. Yurovsky was left alone, but Stalin sent Yurovsky's daughter, Rimma, to the gulags in Siberia where she remained for 25 years. Whatever it was that made Stalin want to have Yurovsky under his absolute control, he certainly came up with a solution that did exactly that. Therefore, we really cannot put together the accounts of these three men, especially since Nikulin was never willing to talk or discuss with anyone what took place that night, so we are left with the opposing statements of Yurovsky and Ermakov. In addition, Yurovsky surrendered his weapon to the museum as the revolver that shot the Tsar. Ermakov also donated his revolver to the museum saying it was the weapon that shot the Tsar. Ermakov gives Yurovsky no big part in the murders, and Yurovsky claims that Ermakov had no major part as he was drunk the entire time. Why is it that these two stories are so opposed, and why their differences as to what happened, which were never resolved, remain part of the mystery of the night? The fourth person, Lyukhanov, is the key as someone who was at the house in the early morning hours of July 17 and stayed with the participants until the morning of July 19 when they say the bodies were buried. He certainly knows what bodies were in the truck, where the truck went, and whether or not it got stuck, and whether the wooden logs were laid down to get the truck out of the mire. Students owe a great debt to Edvard Radzinsky, whose book *THE LAST TSAR,*[83] gives us the first inside look at the truck driver. Lyukhanov was married to the sister of Avdeyev, the prior commandant who got him his job as the chauffeur to the house. His wife was an ardent Bolshevik, much more so than Lyukhanov, and also better educated. In an amazing life story after 1918, Lyukhanov moves from town to town all over Russia, never staying in any one place very long. He received no mention or honors for his participation in the murders. He becomes a cipher in contacting or talking to anyone and with no one contacting or talking to him. In addition, the bedrock of Socialism was, of course, the granting of universal pensions to every man in Russia. He never applied for his pension and never did anything to call attention to himself. His son tells Radzinsky that after the July 17 incident, his father told his mother something he had done that night. His wife, the ardent Bolshevik, was so upset that she left him and never resumed their marriage, even though they had small children. At the end of her life, she told her son that his father was right about what he did, and she was wrong. It is hard to draw any conclusion from that other than the fact that Lyukhanov performed or saw some humane act which involved the Romanovs that was substantial enough that his wife did not continue to remain married to him. The act also must have been serious enough that he disappeared from sight and lived a lonely, poverty stricken life.

An interesting sideline on Lyukhanov appears in the book *A PRISONER OF THE REDS, THE STORY OF A BRITISH OFFICER CAPTURED IN SIBERIA* by Francis McCullagh, where he states: "Of Lyukhanov and his lorry, I have a strange story to tell later." Unfortunately, I can find no evidence that McCullagh told the story.

In the book, on page 164, McCullagh mentions that on the morning of July 18, Lyukhanov brought the truck back to the garage where the person in charge saw the truck bed had been washed with sand and water and was curious about that. Since everyone was aware that the truck had carried the 11 bodies of the recently murdered victims over a 10 mile road, it would not seem "strange" that there was blood in the truck bed. McCullagh states that Lyukhanov was then sent home and didn't participate after that, although every other study shows that Lyukhanov was there until the morning of the 19th.

We do not know, and probably will never know, what it was that was so important, but a possibility is that some or all of the daughters were not killed in the early morning hours of July 17. There are substantial credible witnesses who indicate that it was commonly reported that the daughters had, in fact, been moved. These reports were never given as much credibility as they should have been because all of them had the daughters escaping the murder room, which seemed to be difficult to believe, but if they actually left the house with someone's assistance and Lyukhanov's knowledge of it, or if the Romanov daughters were taken from the house alive in the plan for that night, with the Romanovs and their servants being murdered in different parts of the house at different times, it is not improbable that many different scenarios could have occurred. A question also exists as to whether there was a different result with regard to Maria. Maria was always acknowledged as being the friendliest with the guards. There are numerous instances where Maria talked to the guards about their families and their homes and doing what might be considered as mildly flirting. The story persists that on her 19th birthday on June 23, 1918, a small party was had at the house to celebrate her birthday, and during the course of it, Maria was found in a compromising situation with one of the guards. This was surely nothing more than an embrace or a small kiss, but it would have been an earthshaking event to her parents. Her mother still regarded her daughters as "little girlies" and would have had her Victorian nature shattered by finding that her third daughter had some interest in men. In addition to having this familiarity with a guard, Alexandra would have regarded this as treasonous since the guard was a member of the group that tortured and crucified the Tsar. In his diary, Nicholas makes the typical notation that Maria was 19 today. After that there are six days following where Nicholas made no entry in his diary at all. This was the breaking of the habit of a lifetime, and it may well be explained by what took place on Maria's birthday.

With interest to the question of a missing daughter, when Major Slaughter returned to duty, being stationed in Washington, D.C., several imposters claiming to be children of the Tsar were sent to Major Slaughter, where he acted as the ultimate judge on the person's identity. Several claimants appeared during that period of time, but there was no reasonable claimant pretending to be Nicholas or Alexandra. Claiming to be Alexei was also difficult as the claimant would have had to be a hemophiliac. Therefore, the imposters primarily claimed that they were one of the four daughters of Nicholas and Alexandra. Did Major Slaughter see a daughter while she was still alive? There must have been things the Major saw during his visit into the Ipatiev House, such as the description of the china which was still on the table and the carvings under the dining room table and the physical facts of the house itself and its contents that allowed him to be qualified to question the claimants with enough specificity that he could label the person an imposter. The family has always understood that Major Slaughter was shown some of the bodies of the family. Clearly, he did not see the bodies of four dead daughters or there would have been no need to examine anybody. This again supports the theory that the daughters may have been moved from the house to another location, while one daughter had a brief, temporary escape. Later in life, Major Slaughter insisted that the entire Imperial family was at that point all deceased, the possibility being that he received word that the fourth daughter was captured very quickly and also killed.

SUMMARY

At this point the reader is entitled to have the author assemble the facts and explain what he believes happened to the Romanovs to the best of his ability. It is obvious that conclusions about the Romanov murders become a matter of opinion, and there exists no body of evidence which would lead one to say no reasonable person could conclude that this or that must correctly identify what happened beyond all reasonable doubt.

There would seem to be four possible credible explanations as to what took place during the week of July 14, 1918. The first is that all the Romanovs were murdered in the early morning hours of July 17. The second is that all the Romanovs had escaped sometime during the month of July 1918. The third is that some of the Romanovs were killed but some escaped. The fourth reasonable possibility is that some were killed and some were moved while alive.

What was the situation in Russia in the middle of July 1918? Lenin's hold on the government was very shaky, and Lenin continuously feared that the German government might make some move with respect to Bolshevik Russia. He was concerned that the Germans might station a battalion in Moscow inasmuch as the Germans essentially were able to do whatever they desired regarding Russia. This left Lenin with a problem regarding the Romanovs. The German government continuously made inquiry regarding the condition of the "German Princesses on Russian soil." This phrase leaves some doubt as to how many of the Romanov women were included in the inquiry. Clearly, the German government was concerned about the Empress and her sister, Grand Duchess Ella, as well as the four Romanov daughters.

However, everyone understood that there was a substantial difference in the eventual treatment between the two adult Romanov women as opposed to the four Romanov daughters. At this point Lenin was doing what he did best, which was buying time. His program was shattered when on July 6 a Left Social Revolutionary murdered Count Mirbach, the German ambassador, in his office at the German Embassy. Lenin hastened to do everything possible to maintain his relationship with the German government. If the German government was interested in the possible return to Germany of the Empress and her sister, Ella, it was an unrealistic expectation. The Empress vowed many times never to be rescued by Germany. In addition, the information that the Empress was safe outside Russia would have been a public relations nightmare for Lenin. The Empress was not only the most hated woman in Russia, but she stood as a proxy for the entire Romanov family, as well as being suspected of having German sympathies. Therefore, Lenin's options with respect to the Empress were severely limited. The same was true to a slightly lesser degree with her sister, who had the bad fortune to be the surviving widow of the hated Duke Serge Alexandrovich, as well as the sister of the Empress. The end result appears to be that other than the execution of the Empress and her sister, the Bolsheviks did not kill any other Romanov women, depending on the fate of the four daughters. One reason the daughters may have survived Ekaterinburg is that in 1918 Romanov women had no dynastic importance as they could not inherit the throne.

Many of the possible answers to the fate of the Romanovs have substantial problems. The first solution that all Romanovs were killed in the early morning of July 17 in the Ipatiev House is set forth primarily by the Sokolov book and the Yurovsky Note. Even those who accept those two documents as correct struggle with the problem of 22 people crowded into the small basement room. The fact that they use Sokolov and Yurovsky as the basis for their conclusion leaves that theory gravely damaged. The earlier chapters show the Sokolov account contains not only errors but deliberate misrepresentations of evidence. The Yurovsky Note is such a combination of fact, error, and simply non-credible information that its value is practically nil. Yurovsky's Note as it currently exists simply serves the purpose of allowing the Bolsheviks to say that Sokolov, the White investigator, was correct and keeps them from revealing any additional information. An example of Yurovsky's following of the Sokolov book is exhibited when Sokolov tells us that the Romanovs were lured to the basement room on a "false pretext." Yurovsky's Note then describes how, instead of ordering the Romanovs to the basement room, he delivers a "false pretext," apparently for the reason that that is the only way he is able to get the Romanovs to go to the basement room, which is patently ridiculous. The Romanovs must, of course, go wherever Yurovsky ordered them to go.

The second theory is that all the Romanovs lived to escape during the month of July 1918. This theory has always suffered from the problem that there is no acknowledged, uncontroverted appearance by any of the seven Romanovs in the following 100 years. Explanations are offered as to why the Romanovs needed to remain in hiding, but certainly by the 1960s the reasons they could not make their survival known became very weak. The primary source for the Romanov escape theory is the original book *"RESCUING THE TSAR"* by J.M. Smythe. We have given a detailed study of the book in a prior chapter, and the conclusion that it is absolutely true becomes difficult to sustain. The story of the Romanovs' travel across Siberia simply strains the imagination. The book's main support has been a further book, *"THE HUNT FOR THE TSAR"* by Guy Richards. Mr. Richards accepts the Smythe book as correct, and there is no real question as to Mr. Richards' credibility. However, he acknowledges that there are problems with the escape theory. On page 179 in his book,[84] Mr. Richards states:

> "The evidence pro and con stacks up after 50 years as a kind of Mexican standoff that could give credence to either of the following two contentions:
>
> All members of the Imperial Family were assassinated at Ekaterinburg or all members of the Imperial Family made a secret pre-arranged escape from a staged execution . . . .
>
> Take your choice of the versions.

There is no overwhelming array of proof yet available
to clinch the argument for either side."

Mr. Richards quite honestly explains which theory he accepts but
leaves the ultimate decision up to the reader.

With respect to the theory that some were killed and some escaped,
there is no substantially convincing document that explains how that
occurred, including the description of who was killed and who escaped,
when and to where. The third possibility seems to have very little
chance of being correct. There is very little literature about the fact that
some of the Romanovs may have been killed in the Ipatiev House while
some others may have been moved to another location. This solution is
set forth by Summers and Mangold in THE FILE ON THE TSAR,
but for some reason their evidence concerning the daughters' removal
alive has been largely dismissed or ignored.

What this book does is further the most reasonable solution as to
what happened, taking into account all the problems and the various
evidence and statements. It seems difficult to conclude that if there
were any killings at all, that the three men attendants would not have
been killed at the start. They had no bargaining chip value to the
Bolsheviks, and there would be no concern about their deaths other than
by their families, while allowing them to live would constitute at least
a possible defense force for the women, as well as a simple headache of
handling the men. The most reasonable conclusion is that those three
men were killed at the outset in the basement room. The thought that
the basement room's appearance was simply an effort by the Bolsheviks
to simulate a murder does not seem credible. At that same start, it seems
probable that the Tsar was also executed at that time. He may have been
killed in the basement room or he may have been killed at the separate
execution, neither of which is provable, but it makes no sense to say that
there were killings but the Bolsheviks did not kill the Tsar, who was
essentially the reason for any executions at all.

We propose that three people were killed in the upstairs southeast
bedroom. The substantial proof of that remains the three penciled in
drawings on the upstairs blueprints made on the drawing of the upstairs
by Colonel Slaughter, as well as the photo of blood spatters on the wall

and the location of the Heine poem. There seems to be no acceptable reason why he would have penciled in those three figures other than he knew about and probably saw the three sheet-wrapped bodies there and drew them in on his lecture material blueprints. Slaughter's story of being in the Ipatiev House always has him being shown the upper floor. There is no sensible explanation of the pencil drawn figures being a forgery, as the family has always maintained possession of the slide, and none of them knew that the figures were drawn on there until I advised them of what I found. Obviously, I could not have forged the figures on my copy as the figures appear on the original of Colonel Slaughter's materials which have been and remain in the family's exclusive possession since his death. It then demands a conclusion as to who the three figures in the bedroom are. This study suggested that they are the Empress, whose survival would have been unexplainable to the public by Lenin, as well as her maid, Demidova, killed for the same reason as the three men, and lastly, the Heir Alexei. A reason for the deaths in the upstairs bedroom is that the Empress and Alexei were both barely able to walk or hardly even stand. The conclusion that the Romanovs were killed in separate groups does not have all the problems Yurovsky describes in the 22 person room filled massacre. The Bolsheviks had sufficient manpower to move the Romanovs from room to room or kill them where they were with no difficulties.

This leaves the problem of what took place with respect to the four daughters. Although many people in Russia hated all the Romanovs, their fury seemed to be primarily directed at the Tsar, the Empress, the Tsar's brother, Grand Duke Michael, and the other Romanov Grand Dukes or male members of the family. This is reasonable since the male Grand Dukes' behavior was simply inexcusable, and they quite rightly stood for the excesses of the monarchy. If Nicholas, Alexandra, and Alexei were executed during the week of July 14, what might have happened to the daughters? A reasonable suggestion is that Lenin might well want to keep them alive as a consolation prize for the Germans. The fury of the Russian people did not seem to be specifically directed at the four young girls. Additionally, whatever public relations value could be salvaged from the executions would be substantially helped by the Bolsheviks' explanation that only dynastic members were killed, and they exercised a humane solution with respect to the four young women. This could also explain why in July there was a replacement of Avdeyev with Yurovsky, and also at the last minute the replacement of Ermakov by Yurovsky as head of the execution squad. Yurovsky is obviously much more intelligent and capable than Avdeyev, who was alleged to be an incompetent drunkard. If there was a desire to keep the four daughters alive, someone with the capabilities of Yurovsky would have fitted the escape plan determined by Moscow. Compared to the original nominee to head the executions, who was Peter Ermakov, the choice of Yurovsky makes complete sense. Ermakov was a blood thirsty, vicious, homicidal maniac who would have rebelled at allowing anyone to live. This would also explain why there were so many meetings in Moscow and by the Cheka in Ekaterinburg. It would have been due to trying to reach an agreement between Moscow and Ekaterinburg as to how many of the Romanovs would be killed. Therefore, Ermakov may have been kept away from the Ipatiev House while Yurovsky facilitated Lenin's plan. This also solves one other enduring mystery, which is why the wife of the truck driver, Lyukhanov, who was an ardent Bolshevik, left him after he told her something he did on the execution night. This could only have been some humanitarian act Lyukhanov did with regard to some of the Romanovs which was such a major action that it ended their marriage. The idea that the daughters were taken from the house in Lyukhanov's truck would not only explain Lyukhanov's actions, but the mystery of where the trunk was from midnight until 1:30 a.m. That is only explained by Yurovsky's weak description of why he was unable as commandant of the execution squad to even get a truck sent from the motor pool for over an hour while he waited to perform the most important Bolshevik action imaginable, namely, the execution of the Imperial family. This also dovetails with Summers and Mangold's suggestion that the Romanov daughters lived on in Perm for a number of months after July. By the end of 1918, the daughters essentially served no purpose to Lenin. The Kaiser was exiled and the German government was in collapse. Russia would reclaim all the lands lost to Germany under the Brest-Litovsk Treaty. Most people at this point had assumed that the Romanovs were in fact dead and producing the daughters alive would simply cause complications for Lenin.

Like all solvers of the Romanov murders, this study does not suggest that the above solution is absolutely correct beyond all reasonable doubt. As Mr. Richards stated, there is simply not enough concrete proof to accept one theory and eliminate all the others, but this study does suggest that this solution solves many of the problems that have bedeviled students of the Romanov murders, while retaining the sensible aspects of the physical evidence and the statements of the witnesses.

APPENDIX A

In an attempt to try and reach a consensus about the measurements of the room, particularly the east wall, following is a general discussion of a possible way to try and confirm the room measurements.

Obviously, there is a common sense measurement for the doors on each wall which gives a relationship in the remainder of the room. One method to attempt to reach proportions is to take the wallpaper columns in sets of two, which is one decorated column and one plain column, and attempt to reach the proportions by using those columns. If we count the number of columns from the right edge of the southeast pillar to the left edge of the door frame, there are 9-1/2 sets of columns. By using other general indications of measurement, a figure of 8" per set of two columns seems reasonable. That makes the door 6'4" wide. Starting again at the north edge of the door frame and going north to the south edge of the northeast pillar is 12-1/2 columns, for a measurement of 8'4". This makes a total from the north edge of the southeast pillar to the south edge of the northeast pillar 14'8". It is difficult to determine the measurements of the pillar since the photograph is taken from a straight-on view of the east wall, which makes the side walls appear out of proportion. One measurement of the pillars is said to be 12" square, but that makes the store room doors too narrow. If the west edge of the pillars are each separately over one foot, that makes the room itself between 16' and 17', which seems to be in accordance with many of the measurements.

APPENDIX B

The following are very typical entries for Alexandra's Diary. It is rare for her to refer to any other person with actual details or a detailed description of something that took place that day. The entries frequently contain scripture readings she listened to during the day or a note on the rare occasion when the cook fixed something special.

She will note, "Sunshine after a slight thunder at 3," and the next day "fine weather" and then on June 2, "glorious sunny weather." These are important inasmuch as that is the final entry in her journal for July 16. That entry reads, "10 ½ to bed. 15 degrees." It was very unusual for Alexandra to state "to bed." She frequently will note going to bed, but typical examples are March 18, "Early to bed." March 19, "Worked, early to bed." With the same entry for March 20. May 25 records, "Played bez with Nicholas and then early to bed." The 28th says, "We were in bed by 11." On May 29 Alexandra writes, "I went to bed after supper with strong headache," and then on the next day she writes, "Played bezique with Nicholas before going to bed." The June 3 entry reads, "I played bezique with Nicholas and went to bed at 10. Poured hard in the night." The entry for June 5 is "Played bezique – to bed at 11 (9)." On June 20, it records, "Played bezique with Nicholas and before 11 to bed as very tired." The next entry on the June 24 is, "I went to bed at 10, 22 1/2 ° in the room & 21° outside." The last entry for June 26 is, "I went early to bed, but slept only 3 hours, as they made so much noise outside." July 4 has a typical final entry, "Very hot, went early to bed as awfully tired and heart ached more." There are entries regarding going to bed for July 13, 14, 15, and 16. The 13th states, "I went to bed again." The 14th, "Took a bath & went to bed." The 15th, "Went to bed at 10:15." The final entry on the 16th, of course, is simply "To bed." The diary does not indicate any other occasion in 1918 where she describes her retiring for the night in two words. An example of the colorless entries in this book can be shown by the records for the last half of January. On January 18, she records, "Nicholas read to us." On the 19th, "Nicholas read to us." On the 21st, "Nicholas read to us." These same four words will appear on January 22, 23, 24 25, 27, 28, 29, 30, and 31 and February 1.

APPENDIX C

Sokolov used a great deal of personal interpretation when evaluating a number of items of evidence. Everything that Sokolov regards as meaningful, he can interpret as supporting the basement murder room theory. One of the items on which he bases substantial weight is the Heine poem inscription on the wall of a room in the Ipatiev House.

One of the difficulties with Sokolov's position is that no one knows who wrote the inscription and no one knows when it was written. The basis for Sokolov's theory is the fact that the writer changed the name of the king from "Belshazzar" to "Belsatzar," thereby making it refer to Nicholas II. This causes Sokolov to believe that it must have been an educated Bolshevik who was fluent in German.

There are several things to be noted with respect to the inscription itself. The first is that the end of the first line "selbigen Nacht" partially reappears in the second line where the first and second words are "Van selbigen." The word selbigen in the second line is obviously a mistake and the writer has written the word "seinen" over it, which makes the phrase starting the second line "by his own servants" and, therefore, obviously correct. If someone was copying this inscription from a text, it seems not likely that they would have written the wrong word in the second line as the inscription is very short. The best suggestion is that the writer wrote it from memory and noticed when he finished that he has used the word "selbigen" and corrected the second usage with the one word "seinen." Therefore, we do have to have someone not only fluent in German but who also knew the poem of Heinrich Heine by memory.

The author was also shrewd and witty enough to write the play of letters in the name of Belshazzar.

Although not a handwriting expert, there are certain things that clearly appear from the handwriting on the wall. The first is that both final words in line 1 and line 2 end with the letter "t". The "t" is made in an unusual fashion. The normal writing of the letter "t" is with an upward stroke larger than the small letters in the line and then a downward stroke on the same line followed by a cross bar intersecting the vertical lines about one-fourth from the top. This writer, however, after making the vertical up and down stroke, makes a short line perpendicular to the down stroke about one-third of the way up from the bottom. This unusual letter appears in both lines. In addition, the poem is then ended with a period. There is a period at the end of the second line which seems unneeded.

Can we find any other writing from a person in the area of Ekaterinburg during the period between July 16, 1918 and the discovery of the writing by the second inspector Sergeyev who started his investigation in August 1918? Although there may be numerous comparables, the one that stands out is the signature of the British Agent Robert Bruce Lockhart. Lockhart is one of the brightest and most effective of the British agents. Lockhart's signature on his passport shows the name written in very level script similar to the Heine inscription and the final letter of his name, a "t", is made in exactly the same fashion as the two t's in the Heine inscription, and his signature is then also followed by an unneeded period, so the three t's in the Heine inscription and the passport and the unusual period at the end of both scripts are identical. Sokolov uses the basement wall location of the poem as the final proof of the "basement room" massacre theory of the Romanovs.

Lockhart had substantial opportunity to visit the Ipatiev House between the date of the murders and the time that Judge Sergeyev found the inscription. Certainly the fact that the handwriting closely resembles Lockhart's and the fact that he was in the vicinity and a British agent deeply interested in the fate of the Romanovs is not enough to tie him to the inscription. The connection is made in a biography written by Lockhart entitled BRITISH AGENT and published by G.P. Putnam's

Sons in 1933 in New York and London. In that volume written long after many facts were known dealing with the Romanov murders and the attendant Heine inscription, the author Lockhart writes a passage in dealing with his experiences as a British agent plus a small reference to his student days in Berlin. Lockhart tells us the following: "In Germany a passionate devotion to Heine - even today I can recite by heart most of the Intermezzo and Heimkehr - inspired me." The first curiosity about this passage is why in a biography of his time as a secret agent in Russia he would make a specific note of his student days in Berlin and not only mention the fact that he idolized the poet Heine but that in 1933 he still could repeat from memory large portions of Heine works from his student days in Germany. Lockhart was a very intelligent and very accomplished agent, being David Lloyd George's personal representative to Lenin in Moscow. The fact that he would go to the trouble to include this information in his biography certainly suggests that he wants the reader to discover this clue that he can recite Heine poems from memory, and that fact is important enough to include it in a biography dealing primarily with his work as a British agent. One of the better arguments in favor of Lockhart being the author is that the writer not only knows Heine by memory and is fluent in German, but also is keenly intelligent and has a sense of irony that allows him to compare the Heine poem with the Tsar's death.

It is my hope that this article will encourage someone to investigate the issue in depth and see if it can be ascertained that the Ipatiev House inscription was, in fact, the work of the British Agent Robert Bruce Lockhart.

APPENDIX D

Numerous questions have been raised about Chemodurov and his capabilities. After he was released from prison in the latter part of July 1918, he made a number of statements concerning the whereabouts of the Imperial family. Many of them are in direct contradiction of his other statements. In addition, he gives us no basis for that opinion. Obviously, his knowledge must be second hand as he was confined in prison during the week of July 4, 1918. The question that has been raised is how a man who was interviewed after his release from prison seemed mentally disturbed when two months before he was the closest person in the household to the Tsar. The Tsar and his wife both indicate that they were simply letting the "old" valet have a rest. There is no mention of any problems with his performance of his duties. The valet was in his 60s at the time, which certainly qualifies as old in 1918 Russia. Therefore, how do we account for the difference between his abilities before he went to prison and his mental stability after he is released? Perhaps a possible answer is given by John Sipek, who was a major in the Czechoslovak Army and later Secretary of the Czechoslovak commission representing it in Washington D.C. He was in Perm where he was obtaining a passport when he says that, although his papers were all in order, he was arrested at Perm, taken to Ekaterinburg, and put in prison. He says there were three prisons in Ekaterinburg, and he was in two of them.

In an article in the *New York Times*, published April 6, 1919, Major Sipek gives the following information about treatment of prisoners in the Bolshevik prisons:

"In the daytime life was kind, but in the evening we all felt a little tension. Between 9 and 10 the Bolshevist commission called out those among us who were destined to be placed against the wall that night. It may be imagined that we all listened with considerable interest when the guards began to call out the day's list. Those whose turn did not come for several weeks aged rapidly; young men of 24 looked as if they were 50 years old. I was in that jail approximately 7 weeks, and had 3 different cellmates during that time. One of them was a man 60 years old, who was called out almost every night with a cheerful greeting: 'Put on your coat: It's your turn tonight.' He was led out and an hour later he was brought back with a casual remark that his execution was postponed until tomorrow."

Obviously, there is no proof that that man was Chemodurov, but if that was the type of treatment accorded 60 year old prisoners by the Bolsheviks, there is ample reason to believe that it resulted in the valet's mental disability after his release.

APPENDIX E

Attached hereto are documents from Major Slaughter's military file from the National Archives (NARA) located in Maryland and Missouri. Establishing Major Slaughter's whereabouts during each week of the summer of 1918 is simply not possible. A typical example is the first two documents which are Duty Statements for the year 1918 prepared by Major Slaughter and sent to the Adjutant General of the army. At first glance, they appear to be two copies of the same document, but upon examination, they are, in fact, different. For example, in one document Major Slaughter shows his station as Vladivostok from the period March through September, 1918. In the other document he shows his station for March to May of 1918 as Vladivostok, and then from May to September, in route to Vologda. Frequently, answers from the military in Siberia to inquiries from Washington about Major Slaughter's whereabouts receive answers that simply state, "No news of Slaughter." Very probably there are documents somewhere that were once in Major Slaughter's file, but they are not available to a researcher. Perhaps the best answer to his whereabouts in the summer of 1918 is the army's answer to his wife, who was inquiring about his whereabouts. The army said, "Tell her he is in Siberia."

CHRONOLOGICAL STATEMEN[T] [O]F DUTIES PERFORMED FROM JANUARY 1, [...] TO DECEMBER 31, 1918

DATE FROM—	DATE TO—	STATION	RANK	ORGANIZATION	DUTY	NAME AND RANK OF COMMANDING OFFICERS IMMEDIATE	NEXT SUPERIOR
Jan 1/17	About Apr 1/17	CorregidorPI	1st Lt	13th Inf	Duty MG.Co	Captain W.C.McCaughey	Colonel B.F.Morse
Apr 1/17	May 1/17	Corregidor	1stLt	13th Infantry	Duty MG.Co&Adj try Target Ran	Captain Harris Pendleton	Col B.F.Morse
May 1/17	June 15/17	Corregidor	1stLt	13th Inf	Comdg Hdqrs Co and Adj 13th Inf	Colnel B.F.Morse for both	
June 15/17	July7/17	CorregidorPI	Capt	13thInf	Comdg Co B	Captain Harris Pendleton	Colonel Morse.
July 8/17	July30/17	---------	Capt	15thInf	en route new station--		
July31/17	Sept15/17	TientsinChina	Capt	15thInf	Comdg MG.Co	CaptH.Pendleton &ColW.H.Gordon	Col.Gordon.
Sept15/17	Nov15/17	TientsinChina	Capt	15thInf	Comdg MG.Co & Act JA Amex Chi	Coloel ED.Sigerfoos and palaxinnxkxxxTxWkkmx.	
Nov15/17	Feb 24/18	Tientsin China	Capt	15thInf	Comdg MG.Co	Colonel W.T.Wilder, 15tInf	
Feb 25/18	Mar31/18	en route for change stn.	Capt	15th Inf	AsstMIL ATTACHE Roumania	Travelling War	Dept Or.
Mar31/18	May19/18	Vladivostok	Major	Infantry	Asst Mil Attache Russia,	Col.Ruggles CAC	Col VanDeman
May19/18	Sept/16/18	en route to Vologda Russia	Major	Infantry	Ast Mil Attache Russia	ColRuggles CAC	ColVanDeman
Sep16/18	Sept/23/18	Vladivostok	Major	Infantry	D.S.withAEFSib preparing report	General W.S.Graves	
Sept23/18	Dec31/18	Ekaterinburg& Tchelabinsk R	Major	Infantry	Attached to Czech Staff-Mil Inf and Liason.	General W.S.Graves.	

REMARKS:

In the absence of all records here the forgoing dates in 1917 may be in error to the extent of a week in some cases.

FOREIGN SERVICE:	EUROPE 1917-1918 YRS. MOS. DAYS	SIBERIA 1917-1918 YRS. MOS. DAYS	OTHER 1917-1918 YRS. MOS. DAYS	TOTAL 1917-1918 YRS. MOS. DAY
		0 9 23	1 2 8	2 0 0

Campaigns or Battles Since January 1, 1917: Observed Czech Summer campaign against Bolsheveki along Siberian RailwayJune July and August 1918,Observed Czech and Russian Ural campaign in October,November,and December 1918 including defense Ufa and capture Perm.

Decorations, Special Commendations, Wounds, Etc., Since January 1, 1917:

I Certify that the Foregoing Statements are Correct:

(Signature) H.H.Slaughter,Major Infantry.. (Rank)...........

NOTE: THIS CARD TO BE RETURNED AT ONCE DIRECT TO THE ADJUTANT GENERAL OF THE ARMY.

Form No. 489—A. G. O.
June 7, 1919

(OVER)

128

CHRONOLOGICAL STATEMENT OF DUTIES PERFORMED FROM JANUARY 1, 1918, TO DECEMBER 31, 1918

DATE		STATION	RANK	ORGANIZATION	DUTY	NAME AND RANK OF COMMANDING OFFICER	
FROM —	TO —					IMMEDIATE	NEXT SUPERIOR
Jan 1/17	about Apr 1/17	Corregidor PI	1st Lt	13th Inf	Lt.MG.Co	Capt W.O.McCaughey	Col.B.F.Morse
Apr 1/17	May 1/17	Corregidor PI	1stLt	13th Inf	Duty MG.Co & CampAdjTargetRng	Capt W.O.McCauhey	CaptH.Pendlt
May 1/17	June 14/17	Corregidor	1stLt	13th Ing	ComdgHqr Co & ActRegtlAdj	ColB.F.Morse	Gen.Bailley
June 15/17	July 7/17	Corregidor	Capt	13th Inf	Comd Co.E	Capt H.Pendleton	ColB.F.Morse
July 8/17	July 30/17	------------	Capt	15thInf	en route change station		
Jul 31/17	About Sept 15/17	Tientsin China	Capt	15th Inf	ComdgMG Co.	Capt.H.Pendleton	ColW.H.Gor
Sept 15/17	Nov 15/17	Tientsin China	Capt	15th Inf	Comdg MG Co & ActJAChinaExp.	ColESigerfoos& Col WT Wilder	
Nov 15/17	Mar 8/18	Tientsin Chia	Capt	15th Inf	Comdg MG Co	ColWT Wilder	
Mar8 /18	Mar30/18	Jassy RoumaniA	Capt	15thInf	enroute dutyAst Attache Roumania		
Mar31/18	Sept15/18	Vladivostok	Major	Unassd	AsstMil Attache Russia	ColRuggles C.A.C.	Chief MID War Dept.
Sept16/18	Sept23/18	Vladivostok	Major	Unassd	Duty Hdqrs AEF	Gen WC.Graves	
Sctp24/18	Dec 31/18	Hdqrs Czech Army in Siberia Ekaterinburg and Tchelabinsk	Maj Inf	Unassd	Attached Czech Staff-Mil Inf and LIASON,	Gen WC Graves	

Note: Vladivostok proper station that time I was absent on duty in Siberia for entire period May 19, to Sept-15/18, with Czech Army.

Remarks THE FOREGOING RECORD OF SERVICE IS FROM OLD MEMORANDA AND FROM MEMORY AND WILL IN SOMe CASES BE A FEW DAYS IN ERROR. CERTAIN MINOR DUTIES PERFORMED MAY BE OMITTED. A NEW REPORT WILL BE SUBMITTED AS SOON AS RECORDS BECOME AVAILABLE

Major Infantry UnassD

FOREIGN SERVICE:	EUROPE 1917-1918	YRS.	MOS.	DAYS	SIBERIA 1917-1918	YRS.	MOS.	DAYS	OTHER 1917-1918	YRS.	MOS.	DAYS	TOTAL 1917-1918	YRS.	MOS.	C
							9	22		1	2	8		2	0	0

Campaigns or Battles Since January 1, 1917: With Czech Forces in Siberia, from June 1, 1918 to Sept. 1, 1918 and again attached for duty with The Czechs Siberian Forces From Sept 24, 18 to December 31, 1918. The First duty witnssed the opening of the TranSiberian to Samara, Rus. The latter the retreat of the Czechs from Samara and the Advance beyond Perm.

Decorations, Special Commendations, Wounds, Etc., Since January 1, 1917:

I Certify that the Foregoing Statements are Correct:

(Signature).. (Rank) Major Infantry. Unassd. 5-0796

NOTE: THIS CARD TO BE RETURNED AT ONCE DIRECT TO THE ADJUTANT GENERAL OF THE ARMY.

Form No. 423—A. G. O.
June 7, 1919.

(OVER)

129

SLAUGHTER, HOMER H.
Captain.

File Number.	Date and Name.	Purport of Communication.
2266-H-13	AN-May 4-18	Code tbls.forwdd.---by reli-abl.party yesterday.
2268-165	AK-June 15-18	Understand---now in Russ.
2120-4	MIB-June 22-18 UA***	Req***why.---rept.fully on Russn.rrds.& their condtn.
2235-32	MIB-Aug.8-18. AN*** HA***	---enroute Vologda;no furthr news fr.him.;askg.***keep us informd.
2235-55	AN-Aug.10-18 C.I.Stearns***	---seen by***on his way wit & left him at Omsk. ...cesnd.goods for amb.,to Rusi
2266-I-11	HA-Aug.12-18 Dryscolo. ***	***snw---250 mi.East of Oms k June 9---.
2266-D-53	MIB-Aug.21-18	Req.inf.ref.---locatn.
2229-30	UA-Aug.13-28	Suggests Siberia & rear of Czecho-Slovaks be coverd.by M/A, Peking,or---.
2149-9	IA-Sept.3-18	---to arrive at Irkutsk twn OCTW.
2235-56	MIB-Aug.___-18	---directd.to proceed an further West in Siberia.Cq regtd.to issue ---ars.direc tg.---to rapt.AVP,Siberia.
2266-D-76	UA-July 2-18 Russ.---***	Last nor of---telegram detc Jun to M.Russ.rrds.---A ***Spr***.negotiating with to vis.much.for permission to was thru Japan. Granted. at

SLAUGHTER, HOMER H.
Major.

File Number.	Date and Name.	Purport of Communication.
Personal file 10059-886		
		FINAL REPORT OF---ND GEN GR.WAS FILED IN W.P.D. .NI HISTORICAL SECTION THE .L.C.,G.Q. 3 IN.1
2235-1	ONI-Mar.20-18 MJ.Cutrer***	Advs.has cabled---&***to re main at Vladivostok until further orders.
2235-9	AGO-Mar.26-18	---directd.by SofW take sta tion at Vladivostk.& rept. to M/A,Vologda,Russ.
2291-4	MIB-Mar.23-18	Recoms.---Asst.to M/A Russ be directd.to remn.at Vladi-vostok,pending arvl.of M/A to that point.
2266-D-13	MIB-Apr.3-18	Advises---has no ciph.code.
2003-1007	MIB-Apr.4-18. J.A.Ruggles***	---has bn.made asst.of*** with statn.at Vladivostk.
2268-47	MIB-Apr.25-18	Re Ciph.tbls.2a&2b & 10a&A 10bb being sent---.
2235-17	MIB-Apr.23-18	Recoms.---be detld.in addtn to his other duties sn Actg Quartermaster.
2266-D-29	UA-May7-18	Re departmt.considrg.recom mendatns.to establ.local agt s.important cities Vladivstk disseminate full inf.&to inf uence pub.opinin.,counteract group.from.authorities,etc.

130

March 20, 1918.

My dear Colonel Van Deman:

Confirming our several conversations with Colonel Dunne, a cable message dated March 19th, 1918, has been received from the Commander-in-Chief of the Asiatic Fleet, stating that two officers in the United States Army have reached Vladivostok en route to Roumania, that it was unsafe for them to proceed further, and requesting instructions from the War Department.

To this cable message, the following reply, at your request, has been sent to the Commander-in-Chief of the Asiatic Fleet:

"War Department requests transmission of following instructions: "Notify Major Emile V. Cutrer and Captain Homer H. Slaughter, now at Vladivostok, to remain at that point awaiting further orders. (Signed: Van Deman)."

Very truly yours,

Captain, U. S. Navy,
Assistant Director of Naval Intelligence.

Col. R. H. Van Deman,
Chief, Military Intelligence Section,
Army War College,
Washington, D. C.

131

INDEX SHEET

Chief of Staff - TAG - 3-25-18 211.99 Military Attaches

Sec of War directs that the necessary orders be issued by cable to Capt.

Homer H. Slaughter Infantry, to take station at Vladivostok, reporting

by letter or telegraph to the Military Attache to Russia, Vologda, Russia

Also directing the relief of Major Emile V. Cutrer, Infantry, Vladivostok

Siberia, from duty as assistant to the Military Attache, Jassy Roumania,

and detailing him for duty as an assistant to the Military Attache,

Perking, China reporting for assignment to duty in Peking. WAD*OS 4/12/18

☞ Show from whom, to whom, date, and class number of communication in one line, then drop two spaces and
give a brief synopsis of subject matter, sufficient to identify the document.

FORM NO. 692, A. G. O.
Ed. Jan. 3-18—300,000.

3—5414

201   Index Number
Slaughter, Homer H.
Capt. Inf

INDEX SHEET

Chief of Staff - TAG - 3-25-18   211.99   Military Attaches

Sec of War directs that the necessary orders be issued by cable to Capt.

Homer H. Slaughter Infantry, to take station at Vladivostok, reporting

by letter or telegraph to the Military Attache to Russia, Vologda, Russia

Also directing the relief of Major Emile V. Cutrer, Infantry, Vladivostok

Siberia, from duty as assistant to the Military Attache, Jassy Roumania,

and detailing him for duty as an assistant to the Military Attache,

Perking, China reporting for assignment to duty in Peking. WAD*OS 4/12/18

(Full copy of cablegram sent to Captain Homer H. Slaughter,
Infantry, Vladivostok, Siberia. March 26, 1918. 11:55 P.M.)

Washington, D.C., March 26, 1918.

To Captain Homer H. Slaughter,
    Infantry,
        Vladivostok, Siberia.

        Secretary of War directs you take station at Vladivostok and
report by letter or telegram to American Military Attache to Russia
Vologda, Russia.

                                McCain.

BPK

Copy for:
    Chief War-College Division1

Executive Division.
2235-17

WAR DEPARTMENT
OFFICE OF THE CHIEF OF STAFF
WASHINGTON

April 23 , 1918.

MEMORANDUM FOR THE CHIEF OF STAFF.

> Subject: Detail of Captain Homer H. Slaughter, Inf.,
> an assistant to the Military Attache at
> Russia, stationed at Vladivostok, Siberia,
> as an Acting Quartermaster.

1. Captain Homer H. Slaughter, Infantry, an assistant to the
Military Attache at Russia, is now stationed at Vladivostok, Siberia,
separated from the Military Attache at Vologda, Russia, by several
thousand miles over which transportation is difficult, if not actually
impossible, under present conditions in Russia.

2. It is desired to have this officer open an office in Vladivostok, a locality wherein the importance of prompt information concerning the passing of events is most necessary.

3. In order that this officer may expend funds for rent of office,
make payments for cablegrams, pay his own salary and make such other
disbursements as may be necessary and incident to his detail, it is recommended that he be made, in addition to his other duties, an acting
quartermaster.

4. Memorandum for The Adjutant General of the Army herewith.

> R. H. Van Deman,
> Colonel, General Staff,
> Chief, Military Intelligence Branch,
> Executive Division.

Incl. 1
meh

135

Executive Division.
2235-17

WAR DEPARTMENT
OFFICE OF THE CHIEF OF STAFF
WASHINGTON

April 23 , 1918.

MEMORANDUM FOR THE CHIEF OF STAFF.

Subject: Detail of Captain Homer H. Slaughter, Inf., an assistant to the Military Attache at Russia, stationed at Vladivostok, Siberia, as an Acting Quartermaster.

1. Captain Homer H. Slaughter, Infantry, an assistant to the Military Attache at Russia, is now stationed at Vladivostok, Siberia, separated from the Military Attache at Vologda, Russia, by several thousand miles over which transportation is difficult, if not actually impossible, under present conditions in Russia.

2. It is desired to have this officer open an office in Vladivostok, a locality wherein the importance of prompt information concerning the passing of events is most necessary.

3. In order that this officer may expend funds for rent of office, make payments for cablegrams, pay his own salary and make such other disbursements as may be necessary and incident to his detail, it is recommended that he be made, in addition to his other duties, an acting quartermaster.

4. Memorandum for The Adjutant General of the Army herewith.

R. H. Van Deman,
Colonel, General Staff,
Chief, Military Intelligence Branch,
Executive Division.

Incl. 1
meh

136

EXTRACT OF CABLEGRAM.

OFFICE CHIEF OF STAFF
MIL. INT. BRANCH
EXECUTIVE DIVISION

2266-9-2

Vladivostok,   WAR DEPARTMENT
Dated May 7, 1918.
Received May 8, 1918, 11:30 a.m.

C O D E

Milstaff,

Washington.

No. 2, May 7.

Your May 2 received.

American ambassador telegraphed under date of March 31
food situation Vologda serious and directed food Vladivostok consigned to Riggs be brought Vologda. It is now necessary to go Omsk
and cities west ascertain conditions and report concerning movements
of trains hauling supplies. Request order by cable to take car
loaded food to American ambassador make investigation and return
here. Admiral Knight (?) necessary for this travel.

*   *   *   *   *   *

S L A U G H T E R

meh

137

TELEGRAM

Vladivostok, -3-
Dated May 7, 1918.
No. 2.

Military Information section, G. S. Corps will
be required. Travel direct hereafter. Request
immediate allotment of funds for this purpose
to the amount of $1,000.

S L A U G H T E R.

Copies to:
Chief, War Plans Division.
Chief, Military Intelligence Branch
M. I. 2.

hjn

Approved MAY 17 1918
By order of the Secretary of War

138

WAR DEPARTMENT
EXECUTIVE DIVISION, GENERAL STAFF
MILITARY INTELLIGENCE BRANCH
WASHINGTON

2266-19-28

WAR DEPARTMENT

TELEGRAM

Vladivostok,
Dated May 7, 1918.
Received May 8, 11:30 a. m.

C O D E

Milstaff,

Washington.

No. 2, May 7.

Your May 2 received.

American ambassador telegraphed under date of March 31 food situation Volodga serious and directed food Vladivostok consigned to Riggs be brought Vologda. It is now necessary to go Omsk and cities west ascertain conditions and report concerning movements of trains hauling supplies. Request order by cable to take car loaded food to American ambassador make investigation and return here. Admiral Knight (?) necessary for this travel. Conditions in Siberia (?) (?) Vladivostok. This office (?) Vladivostok is thought likely to become center of great activity Siberia. Will the department consider recommendations to establish local agents important cities Vladivostok disseminate full information, to

Copy to State, C of S, D, WPD, 5/13/18

MAY 17 1918

2266-D-28

WAR DEPARTMENT
OFFICE OF THE CHIEF OF STAFF
WASHINGTON

May 13, 1918

MEMORANDUM FOR CHIEF OF STAFF.

Subject: Delivery of carload of food now at Vladivostok,
Siberia, to American Ambassador at Vologda,
Russia.

1. Herewith is an extract of a cablegram No. 2, dated May 7,
1918, received from the assistant to the Military Attache at Russia,
who is stationed at Vladivostok, Siberia, in which it is stated that
the Ambassador under date of March 31st had telegraphed that the food
situation at Vologda was serious, directing that the food at Vladivostok, consigned to Captain E. Francis Riggs, F. A., an assistant to
the Military Attache to Russia, be brought to Vologda.

2. Captain Slaughter states that it is now necessary to go to
Omsk and cities west to ascertain condition concerning movements of
trains handling supplies. He requests an order by cable to take car
loaded with food to American Ambassador, to make investigation and
to return to Vladivostok. Captain Slaughter states that Admiral Knight
believes this travel to be necessary.

3. It is recommended that this office be authorized to send the
following cablegram to Captain Homer M. Slaughter, Infantry, National
Army, assistant to the Military Attache to Russia stationed at Vladivostok:

"Your No. 2 May 7. Proceed to Vologda with carload
of food which is at Vladivostok consigned to Riggs, delivering consignment to ambassador, and return to proper station.
Cable date of departure and date of return."

meh

R. H. Van Deman,
Colonel, General Staff,
Chief, Military Intelligence Branch,
Executive Division.

Incl. 1

if Ambassador approves

Approved MAY 17 1918
By order of the Secretary of War

140

22LC-O-34

May 20, 1918.

C O D E

Captain Homer H. Slaughter,

care of American Consul,

Vladivostok, Siberia.

7266.O-28

Your No. 2, May 7. Proceed to Vologda with carload of food which is at Vladivostok consigned to Riggs, delivering consignment to ambassador, and return to proper station, if ambassador approves. Cable date of departure and date of return.

Van Deman

mch

SENT

141

May   , 1918.

JUN 1 1918

MEMORANDUM FOR THE ADJUTANT GENERAL OF THE ARMY.

Subject: Detail of Captain Homer H. Slaughter,
Infantry, assistant to the Military
Attache to Russia as Military Observer.

The Secretary of War directs that Captain Homer H. Slaughter,
Infantry, an assistant to the Military Attache to Russia, be
detailed, in addition to his other duties, a Military Observer
with the Armies in Russia.

mch

June 3, 1918.

201. (Slaughter, Homer H.)
Off./ejb/mp/356

American Military Attache,

Petrograd, Russia.
No 25
Captain Homer H. Slaughter, Infantry, in addition to his other duties, is
hereby detailed as a Military Observer with the Armies in Russia.

Cabled June 3, 1918
HLF

Copy sent to the Chief, Army War College Division, Office of the Chief of Staff.

PARAPHRASE

From: Flag Brooklyn, Vladivostock
To: Secnav

    War Department cable May 22nd midnight for Major Slaugh-
ter signed Van Daman un-deliverable, Slaughter left for Volog
May 19th with Colonel Emerson and five assistants of Railroad
Commission.   Major Drysdale , Consul Jamisson, Longdon, Warner
left May 17th for Irkutsk.

                    Flag Brooklyn.

May 1, 1918.

MEMORANDUM FOR THE CHIEF OF STAFF.

Subject: Detail of Captain Homer H. Slaughter, Infantry,
assistant to the Military Attache, Russia, as
a Military Observer.

1.   In Military Intelligence Branch memorandum (MIB 2229-4),
dated April 12, 1918, the Military Attache to Russia, together with
all of his assistants, except Captain Homer H. Slaughter, who is
stationed at Vladivostok, Siberia, were recommended to be made Military Observers for duty with the armies in Russia.

2.   At the time that this memorandum was prepared and forwarded,
Captain Slaughter's name was purposely omitted from the list by reason
of the fact that,he being at Vladivostok, it was thought that conditions were not such as to render it necessary that he be made a
Military Observer at that time.

3.   Since that date, however, the turn of events in eastern
Siberia have made that locality a place of considerable importance.
In addition to this Captain Slaughter has recently left Siberia, taking a carload of food to the American Ambassador at Vologda, Russia,
and it is, therefore, believed that he should be detailed, in addition
to his other duties, a Military Observer with the armies in Russia.

4.   Memorandum for The Adjutant General of the Army and draft
of letter from the Secretary of War to the Secretary of State herewith.

R. H. Van Deman,
Colonel, General Staff,
Chief, Military Intelligence Branch,
Executive Division.

Incls. 2
meh

145

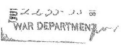

In reply refer to
Di 121.54/1063.

June 11, 1918.

The Secretary of State presents his compliments to
the Honorable the Secretary of War and, acknowledging
the receipt of his letter (MIB 2235-29) of the 1st instant,
has the honor to advise him that the information contained
therein, that in addition to his other duties Captain Homer
H. Slaughter, Infantry, Assistant to the American Military
Attaché to Russia, has been detailed by the War Department
as a Military Observer with the armies in Russia, has been
duly noted in the Department of State and communicated to
the American Ambassador at Vologda, Russia.

ASSISTANT AND CHIEF CLERK
JUN 13 1918
WAR DEPT.

REC'D M.I.B. O.C.S.

TELEGRAM

Murmansk, -5-
Dated July 9, 7 p. m.
No. 66.

of men. According to one report which probably somewhat exaggerated 700,000 Poles taken to Germany as
laborers.

8. Above cabled Pershing in my No.
155, July 9, 7 p. m.

9. With reference to paragraphs 15
and 16. See my No. 57, June 26, 5 p. m. and 24, May
10, 2 p. m.

French are in direct touch with
Czecho-Slovak organization and we benefit indirectly.

10. Reference paragraph 17. Last
news of Slaughter telegram dated June 19 received
June 26 from station Miass near Zlanoust,
Gfimskaya government. He and Emerson and party then
negotiating with soviet authorities for permission
to pass through lines. Later not signed telegram
from Perm received by embassy from Urzhoumka June
28 seems to indicate permission granted and party
now

TELEGRAM

Murmansk,   -6-
Dated July 9, 7 p. m.
No. 66.

now en route here. Will advise by cable upon receipt
of further news.

R U G G L E S.

hjn

149

WAR DEPARTMENT TELEGRAM.

OFFICIAL BUSINESS

WASHINGTON.   August 8, 1918.

2235-

IG 10

WAR DEPARTMENT

CODE

American Military Attache,

Tokio, Japan.

Capt. Slaughter on route to Vologda wired us May 29 from Krasnoyark. Have had no further news from him. Make effort to locate him. Keep us informed. Same request to China.

Walter F. Martin CHURCHILL
Lieut. Colonel, Cavalry, U.S.A.

meh

Am.
Send same cable to/Military Attache, Peking, China.

SENT

TELEGRAM

WAR DEPARTMENT

Tokio.

Dated August 10, 1918.

Received Aug.10, 6:25 a.m.

CODE.

Milstaff,
Washington.

No. 87, August 10, 11 a.m.

Col. Steward, Russian railroad service corps,
now in United States left Slaughter at Omsk in June.
I understand Slaughter was proceeding to Russia with
canned goods and supplies for American ambassador on
the same train as Col. Emerson. Steward returned
via Amur railroad line and reached Vladivostok July 9.

B A L D W I N.

rrs

CONFIDENTIAL COPIES TO:
Chief of Staff   W. P. D.   State Dept.   Cable Office   M. I. 2.   Capt. Martin
        8/10/18

151

WESTERN UNION
TELEGRAM

CLASS OF SERVICE	
Telegram	
Day Letter	Blue
Night Message	Nite
Night Letter	N L

If none of these three symbols appears after the check (number of words) this is a telegram. Otherwise its character is indicated by the symbol appearing after the check.

NEWCOMB CARLTON, PRESIDENT   GEORGE W. E. ATKINS, FIRST VICE-PRESIDENT

CLASS OF SERVICE SYMBOL	
Telegram	Blue
Day Letter	Blue
Night Message	Nite
Night Letter	N L

If none of these three symbols appears after the check (number of words) this is a telegram. Otherwise its character is indicated by the symbol appearing after the check.

RECEIVED AT WYATT BUILDING, COR. 14TH AND F STS., WASHINGTON, D. C. ALWAYS OPEN

2526P XA 27 NL 3 EX

S SANFRANCISCO CAL AUG 29 1918

ADJUTANT GENERAL 11031

US ARMY WASHN DC

PLEASE TELL ME WHEREABOUTS OF MY HUSBAND MAJOR H H SLAUGHTER
INFANTRY HEARD LAST JUNE 8 EASTERN SIBERIA

MRS H H SLAUGHTER STEWART HOTEL SANFRAN

25   Received A G O AUG 30 1918   1050P

Maj. Homer H. Slaughter, Inf.
Vladivostok, Siberia.

Detailed as Military Observer with
Armies in Russia June 3/18

Aug. 30/18   Returned Farrow
                                      M.A.

Maj. McNeill—
    8/31 Shall information be given?

    Tell him he is in
    Siberia. 8/31 C.N.M.

153

INDEX SHEET

AG 370.22 Russian Exped.   10-6-18

C.G., AEF in Siberia   T A G

Enclosing copy of report from Maj. Slaughter, who went west from Vladivostok with General Gaida.   Also report relative to the attitude of the Allied Commanders in Russia toward the U.S.

mc/mcm   6-24-20

☞ Show classification number and date of communication on first line, drop two spaces, show source of communication and to whom addressed, then drop two spaces again and give a brief synopsis of subject matter sufficient to identify the document.

Form No. 622, A. G. O.
Feb. 25-19.

a 2—0414

September 1918.

MEMORANDUM FOR THE ADJUTANT GENERAL OF THE ARMY.

Subject: Orders relieving Major Homer H. Slaughter, Infantry, U. S. A., from duty as Assistant Military Attache to Russia, and directing him to report to the Commanding General, American Expeditionary Forces, Siberia, for duty.

1.   The Secretary of War directs that Major Homer H. Slaughter, Infantry, U. S. A., stationed at Vladivostok, Siberia, and reported on September 9, 1918, to be at Irkutsk, Siberia, be relieved from duty as Assistant to the Military Attache to Russia and that he be directed by cable to report to the Commanding General, American Expeditionary Forces, Siberia for duty.

FRANK McINTYRE,
Major General, General Staff Corps,
Executive Assistant to Chief of Staff.

rc

155

C O D E

American Military Attache,
     Peking, China.

     If you can communicate with Slaughter at Irkutsk direct
him not to proceed any further West in Siberia. Chief of Staff has
been requested to issue orders directing Slaughter to report to
Commanding General, United States Expeditionary Forces, Siberia.
Report cable steps taken by you to comply with the foregoing.

                                   C H U R C H I L L

     By:

          Walter F. Martin,
     Lt. Colonel, Cavalry, U. S. A.

     rg

W. D., STANDARD
FORM NO. 12.

                                             time his journey to
                                          stant Military Attache
                                          no longer necessary.

                                          ted in the memorandum
                         General of the Army herewith.

Additional record
A. G. O.   8454   a letter from The Secretary of War to The
        7/31/19   to herewith.

No. 124-1, A. G. O.

                                        M. Churchill,
                               Brigadier General, General Staff,
                               Director of Military Intelligence.

     2 encls.
     rg

WAR DEPARTMENT
OFFICE OF THE CHIEF OF STAFF
WASHINGTON.

September 9, 1918.

MEMORANDUM FOR LIEUT. NELSON.

Miss Gould will give you the cable just sent to the Military Attache, Peking, and Colonel Dunn wishes a memorandum submitted to the Chief of Staff defining the present status of Slaughter and how he was directed by the Ambassador to proceed with a carload of food and why the necessity for his being with the Ambassador no longer exists.

Colonel Dunn wishes us to state in this memorandum that we request that Slaughter be relieved as Military Attache and that he be directed by cable to report to the Commanding General of the American Expeditionary Forces in Siberia for duty in the Intelligence section under his forces.

Walter F. Martin,
Lt. Colonel, Cavalry, U. S. A.

rg

September 17, 1918.

A.G.201,Slaughter,H.H.
Offrs.358,ejb/mm   The

Commanding General, Amexforce, Vladivostok.
    Number 19
            Order made relieving Major Homer H. Slaughter, Infantry,
duty Assistant Military Attache to Russia, and directing him report
to Commanding General, Amexforce, Siberia, for duty.

Cabled Sept 17, 1918
            HLF

TELEGRAM

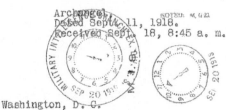

Archangel,
Dated Sept. 11, 1918.
Received Sept. 18, 8:45 a. m.

NOTED: M, G.2.

<u>C O D E</u>

Milstaff,

Washington, D. C.

No. 85, September 11, 2 p. m.

Allied and Russian troops have taken
Obozerskaya 225 miles south on Archangel railroad.
Land wire connecting that with Murmansk line, and
will be put in service as soon as possible.

Your telegram referring to my No.
80, paragraphs 4A, 5A, 6A, and requiring explanation
for failure to comply with certain instructions was
received with delay and no number, also garbled as
have been practically all cablegrams received past.
No instructions ever received by me were understood
to prohibit suggestions concerning military matters,
but prohibiting me here requesting information as to
American policy in Russia, direct me to get this from
ambassador.

TELEGRAM

Archangel,   -2-
Dated Sept. 11, 2 p. m.
No. 85.

Your orders are now understood.

(*) with Martin is by wire and

courier, the former very uncertain with long delay.

Mail may be forwarded via Murmansk.

My No. 78 and 79 repeated yesterday.

No. news of Slaughter.

R U G G L E S.

hjn

160

OFFICE OF THE CHIEF OF STAFF
WASHINGTON. AND
JOHN M. DUNN

WAR DEPARTMENT

September   , 1918.

MEMORANDUM FOR THE CHIEF OF STAFF.

Subject: Orders relieving Major Homer H. Slaughter,
            Infantry, U. S. A., from duty as Assistant
            to the Military Attache to Russia, and
            directing him to report to the Commanding
            General, American Expeditionary Forces,
            Siberia, for duty.

1.   In a memorandum for the Chief of Staff dated May 13,
1918, file No. MID 2266-D-28, this office requested authority
to direct Major Homer H. Slaughter, Infantry, U. S. A., to
proceed from Vladivostok, Siberia, to Vologda, Russia, with a
carload of food consigned to the American Ambassador. This
memorandum was approved, and on May 20, 1918 Major Slaughter
was cabled to proceed to Vologda.

2.   In June, Major Slaughter was heard of at Omsk, but
due to the extraordinary conditions prevailing in Siberia, he
was apparently unable to proceed farther.

3.   The following cablegram dated September 8, 1918, has
been received from our Military Attache, Peking, China:

        "Major Slaughter to arrive at Irkutsk tomorrow."

From the above it is clear that Major Slaughter has found it
necessary to retrace his steps from Omsk.

4.   In view of the recent turn of events in Russia and the
sending of an American Expeditionary Force to Siberia, it is
impracticable for Major Slaughter to continue his journey to
Vologda, and it is believed that an Assistant Military Attache
to Russia with station at Vladivostok is no longer necessary.

5.   Action is recommended as indicated in the memorandum
for the Adjutant General of the Army herewith.

6.   Draft of a letter from The Secretary of War to The
Secretary of State herewith.

                        M. Churchill,
                Brigadier General, General Staff,
                Director of Military Intelligence.

2 encls.
rg

161

APPENDIX F

During the period from Nicholas II's abdication in March 1917 until his execution in July 1918, the clocks and calendars in Russia were in a state of flux. Not only in Russia, but in other countries, there was a difference on any given day between those countries that used the Julian calendar and those that used the Gregorian calendar. Those using the Gregorian calendar found that they were 12 days ahead of the countries that used the Julian calendar. Russian officials began the use of the Gregorian calendar in February 1918. Therefore, Russia had to make up 13 days that they would be missing in the Julian calendar. After February 1918, it was common for people, including Nicholas and Alexandra, to use both dates in written documents in the following manner: 2/15. It was also common to write the dates as 2 OS, meaning old style, and then 15 NS, meaning new style.

Combined with this was the confusion as to a standard time in different parts of Russia, since Russia even today contains many different time zones. The difference between the time in Ekaterinburg and in Moscow and in St. Petersburg varied according to the time zone. When it was 6 p.m. in St. Petersburg, it would be 6:30 p.m. in Moscow and 8 p.m. in Ekaterinburg. In addition, on June 1, 1918, daylight savings time was ordered in effect in Russia, which meant that all clocks should be changed by two hours. This was honored in some areas and ignored in other areas. Further adjustment must be noted with respect to telegrams sent to the government in Moscow. It was generally the practice that those telegrams would be time stamped at the time in Moscow and not the time in the area from which the telegram was sent.

Lastly, Bolsheviks' accounts of July 1918 constantly refer to the need to accomplish something before daylight or to start something after daylight. Attached hereto is a time schedule showing the amount of light available in Ekaterinburg on July 16, 17 and 18, 1918.

Ekaterinburg (56°50'N 60°35'E)

July 16, 1918

3:27 a.m.: begin civil twilight (sun is just below the horizon and there is generally enough light to carry out most outdoor activities)

4:26 a.m.: sunrise

2:25 p.m.: moonrise

9:39 p.m.: sunset

10:38 p.m.: end civil twilight (after this time, most outdoor activities require some degree of artificial light)

11:26 p.m.: moonset

July 17, 1918

3:29 a.m.: begin civil twilight (sun is just below the horizon and there is generally enough light to carry out most outdoor activities)

4:28 a.m.: sunrise

3:28 p.m.: moonrise

9:38 p.m.: sunset

10:36 p.m.: end civil twilight (after this time, most outdoor activities require some degree of artificial light)

11:46 p.m.: moonset

July 18, 1918

3:31 a.m.: begin civil twilight (sun is just below the horizon and there is generally enough light to carry out most outdoor activities)

4:30 a.m.: sunrise

4:41 p.m.: moonrise (waxing gibbous: 60% of moon's visible disk illuminated)

9:37 p.m.: sunset

10:34 p.m.: end civil twilight (after this time, most outdoor activities require some degree of artificial light)

July 19, 1918

12:11 a.m.: moonset

3:34 a.m.: begin civil twilight (sun is just below the horizon and there is generally enough light to carry out most outdoor activities)

4:31 a.m.: sunrise

5:50 p.m.: moonrise

9:35 p.m.: sunset

10:32 p.m.: end civil twilight (after this time, most outdoor activities require some degree of artificial light)

July 20, 1918

12:46 a.m.: moonset

APPENDIX G

As to the major question of when, where, and how the Tsar's death occurred, one is required to look at numerous other side issues in the hope that they may at least shed some light on the question. One of these is the issue of the famous telegram of July 17, 1918, which was sent from Ekaterinburg presumably intended for Moscow. The telegram says: "Tell Sverdlov entire family suffered same fate as head officially family will die in evacuation." Much effort has been spent on considering individual words and phrases in the telegram in an attempt to glean more information that might shed light on the murders. Again, Summers and Mangold are the first persons to conduct a physical, scientific evaluation of the telegram. They raise the question that the sender's name "Beloborodov" appears at the bottom of the telegram blank, but it is written in script while the rest of the body of the telegram is typed. That raises the question whether this is an authenticate signature of Beloborodov or not. Presumably, there are four possibilities: First, the telegram and the signature are genuine. Second, the body of the telegram is genuine but the signature was added by someone else at Beloborodov's instruction. Third, the body of the telegram is genuine but Beloborodov's signature was forged without his consent. Fourth, the entire telegram and signature are a forgery. It is helpful in studying the telegram blank to note that many pictures of the telegram show a more or less pristine copy with all four edges being sharp and undamaged. The actual telegram shows damage to the edges of the telegram which gives rise to further questions about how it was handled from the time it left the telegraph office forward. It should be compared with another telegram also sent from Ekaterinburg which is dated July 17, 1918. In examining the two blanks used to type the messages, the top part of the form is an area where the person physically sending the telegram fills in various number and information. On the right hand side of the area and on the entire area in the second telegram there are numbers hastily scribbled in pencil. The penciled area on the second telegram is basically unreadable and is simply information by the clerk regarding the sending of the telegram. If you inspect the July 17 telegram, you will note that the left two-thirds of the telegram are not filled in by the pencil scribbling clerk but are neatly filled in what would appear to be black ink. The importance of this is that just under the line before the typed message are a few letters also in blank ink and all of those writings appear to have been done with the same ink in the writing instrument used in Beloborodov's signature. What would that prove? It might well indicate that the message was typed in advance but not sent immediately and that later Beloborodov instructed a different and perhaps higher placed official in the telegraph office to fill in the remaining part of the information in the top box and also affix his name at the bottom in that he had not dictated a signature when the rest of the telegram was dictated.

Could this situation have reasonably occurred on the evening of July 17? At that time Beloborodov had just finished having his order carried into fruition by killing the Tsar of all the Russias and his family. Beloborodov is certainly entitled to some anxiety and forgetfulness under the circumstances. This telegram is not a later formal report but sent on the spur of the moment by Beloborodov. The other possibility is the message in the telegram was, in fact, typed and not sent and that later an unauthorized person filled in the needed data on the left to show the telegram sent and added Beloborodov's signature, making a genuine, but unsent, telegram message finished by adding a fraudulent signature. Obviously, a more scientific examination can give us further detailed information about the above.

BIBLIOGRAPHY

Books

Ackerman, Carl W. *Trailing the Bolsheviki: Twelve Thousand Miles with the Allies in Siberia* (1919), New York: Charles Scribner's Sons, 1919.

Alexandrov, Victor. *The End of the Romanovs*, translated by William Sutcliffe, Boston: Little, Brown and Company, 1966.

Bernstein, Herman. *The Willy-Nicky Correspondence*, New York: Alfred A. Knopf, 1918.

Buchanan, George. *My Mission to Russia and Other Diplomatic Memories* [Volume 1], General Books.

Buchanan, George. *My Mission to Russia and Other Diplomatic Memories* [Volume 2], General Books.

Bulygin, Captain Paul and Kerensky, Alexander. *The Murder of the Romanovs: The Authentic Account*, Westport, CT: Hyperion Press, 1975.

Buxhoeveden, Baroness Sophie. *Left Behind: Fourteen Months in Siberia During the Revolution, December 1917 – February 1919*, London: Longman's Green and Company, 1929.

Bykov, P.M. *The Last Days of Tsardom*, translated by Andrew Rothstein, London: Martin Lawrence Ltd., 1934.

d'Encausse, Hélène Carrère. *Nicholas II: The Interrupted Transition*, translated by George Holoch, New York: Holesm & Meier, 2000.

Erickson, Carolly. *Alexandra: The Last Tsarina*, New York: St. Martin's Press, 2001.

Ferro, Marc. *Nicholas II: The Last of the Tsars*, translated by Brian Pearce, New York & Oxford: Oxford University Press, 1993.

Francis, David Rowland. *Russia from the American Embassy, April, 1916 – November, 1918*, New York: Charles Scribner's Sons, 1921.

Gelardi, Julia P. *From Splendor to Revolution: The Romanov Women, 1847-1928*, New York: St. Martin's Press, 2011.

Gerard, James W. *Face to Face with Kaiserism*, New York: George H. Doran Company, 1918.

Gilliard, Pierre. *Thirteen Years at the Russian Court*, London: Hutchison & Co., 1923.

Graves, Dr. Armgaard Karl. *The Secrets of the German War Office*, New York: McBride, Nast & Company, 1914.

Hyde, Christopher. *The House of Special Purpose*, New York: New American Library, 2004.

Kennan, George F. *Soviet-American Relations, 1917-1920, Volume 1: Russia Leaves the War*, Princeton, New Jersey: Princeton University Press, 1956.

Kerensky, Alexander. *The Murder of the Romanovs*, Westport CT: Hyperin Press, Inc.

King, Greg. *The Court of the Last Czar: Pomp, Power, and Pageantry in the Reign of Nicholas II*, Hoken, NJ: John Wiley & Sons, 2006.

King, Greg and Wilson, Penny. *The Fate of the Romanovs*, Hoboken, NJ: John Wiley & Sons, 2003.

Klier, John & Mingay, Helen. *The Quest for Anastasia: Solving the Mystery of the Lost Romanovs*, Secaucus, NJ: Carol Publishing, 1997.

Levine, Isaac Don. *Eyewitness to History: Memoirs and Reflections of a Foreign Correspondent for Half a Century*, New York: Hawthorne Books, 1973.

Lockhart, R.H. Bruce. *British Agent*, New York: G.P. Putnam's Sons, 1933.

Lovell, James Blair. *Anastasia: The Lost Princess*, Washington, D.C.: Regnery Gateway, 1991.

Maples, William R. PhD. and Browning, Michael. *Dead Men Do Tell Tales*, New York: Doubleday, 1994.

Maylunas, Andrei & Mironenko, Sergei. *A Lifelong Passion: Nicholas and Alexandra Their Own Story*, translated by Darya Galy, London: Weidenfeld & Nicolson, 1996.

McCullagh, Francis. *A Prisoner of the Reds, the Story of a British Officer Captured in Siberia*, London: John Murray, 1921.

McNeal, Shay. *The Secret Plot to Save the Tsar: The Truth Behind the Romanov Mystery*, New York: HarperCollins, 2001.

Moorehead, Alan. *The Russian Revolution*, New York: Harper & Brothers, 1958.

Nicholas & Alexandra: The Last Imperial Family of Tsarist Russia, New York: Harry N. Abrams, 1998.

O'Conor, John F. *The Sokolov Investigation*, London: Souvenir Press, 1972.

Perry, John Curtis & Pleshakov, Constantine. *The Flight of the Romanovs: A Family Saga*, New York Basic Books, 1999.

Potts, D.M. and Potts, W.T.W. *Queen Victoria's Gene: Haemophilia and Royal Family*, Thrupp, Gloucestershire, England: Sutton Publishing, 1995.

Preston, Thomas. *Before the Curtain*, London: John Murray, 1950.

Rappaport, Helen. *The Last Days of the Romanovs*, NY: St. Martin's Press, 2008.

Richards, Guy. *The Hunt for the Czar*, Garden City, NY: Doubleday & Company, 1970.

Rounding, Virginia. *Alix and Nicky: The Passion of the Last Tsar and Tsarina*, New York: St. Martin's Press, 2011.

Slaughter, Stephen S. *History of a Missouri Farm Family: The O.V. Slaughters, 1700-1944*, Harrison, New York: Harbor Hill Books, 1978.

Smythe, James P. *Rescuing the Czar*, Chennai, India: Tutis, 2007.

Sokolov, Nicholas A. *The Sokolov Investigation of the Alleged Murder of the Russian Imperial Family*, translated by John F. O'Conor, London; Souvenir Press, 1972.

Sokoloff, Nicolas. *Enquête Judiciare Sur L'Assassinat de la Famille Impériale Russe*, Paris: Payot, 1926; Russian edition.

Steinberg, Mark D. and Khrustalëv. *The Fall of the Romanovs*, New Haven, CT: Tale University Press, 1995.

Summers, Anthony and Mangold, Thomas. *The File on the Tsar*, New York: Harper & Row, 1976.

Telberg, George Gustav. *The Last Days of the Romanovs*, New York: George H. Doran & Co., 1926.

Wilton, Robert. *The Last Days of the Romanovs*: *How the Tsar Nicholas II and Russia's Imperial Family Were Murdered*, Newport Beach, CA: Institute for Historical Review, 1993.

Newspapers

Sipek, John. "Is the Ex-Czar Still Living?" *New York Times*, April 6, 1919.

Announcement of the Tsar's Death. *New York Times*, July 20, 1918.

Herman Bernstein, Death of the Tsar. *New York Times*

Periodicals

Assembly, United States Military Academy at West Point, New York. Slaughter obituary, October 1955.

Worker Revolution in the Urals, by P.M. Bykov, published 1921.

ENDNOTES

1   Sokolov, Nicholas A. *The Sokolov Investigation of the Alleged Murder of the Russian Imperial Family*, translated by John F. O'Conor, Souvenir Press, London, 1972; French edition: Paris: Payot, 1926; Russian edition: Slowo, Berlin, 1925.

2   O'Conor, John F. *The Sokolov Investigation*, Souvenir Press, London, 1972.

3   Summers, Anthony and Mangold, Thomas. *The File on the Tsar*, Harper & Row, New York, 1976.

4   Radzinsky, Edvard. *The Last Tsar*, Doubleday, New York, 1992.

5   King, Gregory and Wilson, Penny. *The Fate of the Romanovs*, John Wiley & Sons, Hoboken, NJ, 2003.

6   McNeal, Shay. *The Secret Plot to Save the Tsar: The Truth Behind the Romanov Mystery*, Harper Collins, New York, 2001. This book completely destroys the old story that King George V made no effort at all to try and help or rescue his Russian relatives.

7   Rappaport, Helen. *The Romanov Sisters*, St. Martin's Press, New York, 2014.

8   A morganatic marriage occurred when a person of royal status married someone who was not royal. The result would normally be that the non-royal spouse would not take a style or title of the royal spouse, which would normally occur, and neither would their children.

9   Natasha (Natalie) Wulfert was the daughter of a middle class Moscow lawyer. She first married a man named Mamantov with whom she had a daughter, but the marriage ended in divorce. She very quickly married her second husband, Lt. Wulfert, an officer in the Imperial Guard Calvary. She was still married to Lt. Wulfert at the time she began her affair with Grand Duke Michael.

10 The Grand Duchess Vladimir, usually known as Marie Pavlovna, the Elder, suddenly found that her sons were closer to inheriting the throne than anybody would have thought likely. Consequently she quickly converted to

Orthodoxy, but the marital religious problem still constituted difficulty with inheriting the throne

11   The Duma was and still is Russia's parliament. The Duma was organized as the Russian parliament as a result of the Revolution of 1905. Nicholas very grudgingly gave into the advice of his counsellors and agreed that Russia could have a parliament consisting of elected members; however, Nicholas reserved the right to disband the Duma at any time, which he did, meaning that their existence was essentially worthless.

12   The Grand Duke was probably the most despised member of all the grand dukes. He was haughty, severe and often rude. He was a believer in the absolute authority of the monarchy. He was married to the Empress's beautiful sister Ella, but the marriage was apparently one of form only.

13   King, Gregory and Wilson, Penny. *The Fate of the Romanovs*, John Wiley & Sons, Hoboken, NJ, 2003, p.55.

14   The only time Nicholas entered a diary entry showing his personal feelings was on the date that the Bolsheviks made him remove his epaulets. Nicholas in a rare show of emotion calls the Bolsheviks "swine."

15   Crawford, Rosemary and Donald. *Michael and Natasha*, Alisa Drew Book/ Scribner, New York, 1997.

16   Alexander Kerensky, an attorney, was a member of the first government and served as Minister of Justice. Kerensky, by force of his personality, took charge and soon became the leading figure of the new government.

17   Summers, Anthony and Mangold, Thomas. *The File on the Tsar*, Harper & Row, New York, 1976, p. 39.

18   Yakolev, like many figures in this period, remains a person of mystery. There were allegations that he was a secret monarchist or that he was a German agent or that he was a double agent. He is sometimes identified by the previous name Miachin. Proof of his identity remains vague.

19   Alexei and his three sisters and their attendants were finally transferred from Tobolsk to Ekaterinburg on May 23, 1918.

20   The house was completely demolished by orders of the Central Government in 1977. The demolition was in the charge of the ranking local governmental official for the area, namely: Boris Yeltsin.

21   Nicholas Ipatiev was a wealthy mining engineer in the City of Ekaterinburg, which was located in the dense mineral area of the Ural Mountains. He surrendered the house immediately upon demand by the Bolsheviks and would later regain possession of the house after the Bolsheviks fled Ekaterinburg.

22   Mr. Radzinsky was doing research in the Russian archives when to his surprise he found a folder labeled Romanov File. There was not supposed to be any such file in the archives. On opening the file Mr. Radzinsky

discovered that it contained the Yurovsky Note. The circumstances regarding the appearance of the file and the Note remain unclear.

23 *The Last Diary of Tsaritsa Alexandra*. Edited by VA Kozlov and VM Khrustalëv. Yale University Press, New Haven and London, 1997.

24 *The Last Diary of Tsaritsa Alexandra*. Edited by VA Kozlov and VM Khrustalëv. Yale University Press, New Haven and London, 1997. Pgs. 193, 194, 195, 196, 197. "Remained in bed all day, I spent the day on my bed, spent the day as yesterday lying in the bed, spend the day on the bed again, lay on my bed again." The above are Alexandra's diary entries for July 11 through July 15, 1918. At this point Alexandra was essentially bedfast.

25 The Bolsheviks sent letters to the family purportedly from a loyal officer in order to trap the family into replying so the Bolsheviks would have proof of an attempted escape. On one letter it has been amended by the family, probably by Olga, to show their regular bedtime as 11:30 and not 10:30 as the Bolshevik letter showed.

26 King, Gregory and Wilson, Penny. *The Fate of the Romanovs*, John Wiley & Sons, Hoboken, NJ, 2003, p. 107.

27 Michael Letemin was a house guard who apparently took a huge number of items from the house and also took Alexei's dog, Joy, to his house where the dog was recovered by the British.

28 O'Conor, John F. *The Sokolov Investigation*, Souvenir Press, London, 1972, p. 31.

29 Telberg, George. *The Last Days of the Romanovs*, George H. Doran Company, New York.p. 160.

30 Summers, Anthony and Mangold, Thomas. *The File on the Tsar*, Harper & Row, New York, 1976. In 1937 a German Court gave the surviving Romanov relatives the right to divide a small inheritance. Anna Anderson, the long-time "Anastasia" impersonator, would also bring suit which was in court on October 15, 1957. The suit had been interrupted by WW II and it would continue and continue until the court finally concluded that it could find neither that Anastasia was dead or that Anna Anderson was Anastasia.

31 Summers, Anthony and Mangold, Thomas. *The File on the Tsar*, Harper & Row, New York, 1976. p. 133

32 Telberg, George. *The Last Days of the Romanovs*, George H. Doran Company, New York.

33 O'Conor, John F. *The Sokolov Investigation*, Souvenir Press, London, 1972, p. 108.

34 O'Conor, John F. *The Sokolov Investigation*, Souvenir Press, London, 1972, p. 109.

35 O'Conor, John F. *The Sokolov Investigation*, Souvenir Press, London, 1972, p. 116.

36 O'Conor, John F. *The Sokolov Investigation*, Souvenir Press, London, 1972, p. 126

37 Collins Gem Russian Dictionary. William Collins Sons & Co. Ltd., 1963.

38 Collins Gem Russian Dictionary. William Collins Sons & Co. Ltd., 1963.

39 Old Testament, Book of Daniel, Chapter 5, verses 1-30.

40 Smythe, James P. *Rescuing the Tsar*, Chennai, India, Tutis, 2007.

41 *The Willy-Nicky Correspondence*. Knoff, Alfred A. publisher, New York, 1918. This volume is a compilation of the letters between Kaiser Wilhelm II and Nicholas II. The introduction was written ty Theodore Roosevelt, who calls Nicholas a "poor, feeble puppet."

42 Barton, George. *Celebrated Spies and Famous Mysteries of the Great War*, Page Company, New York, 1919.

43 Sergeyev has with him his original file when he is interviewed by Bernstein, and is very explicit about finding the poem in the upstairs southeast bedroom.

44 Sokolov, Nicholas A. *The Last Days of the Romanovs*, Slowo, Berlin, 1925.

45 At this point news of the Tsar's death had begun to appear in international papers, including the announcement in *The New York Times*.

46 Herman Bernstein was a very respected reporter for *The New York Times*. He did not believe the Sokolov account of the murders. Consequently, he later contacted Judge Sergeyev who had a file on his investigation. He went over the file with Mr. Bernstein, and the judgments of Judge Sergeyev again cast doubt on the Sokolov report.

47 Grand Duchess Ella was born Princess Elizabeth of Hesse and was an older sister of the Empress. She had previously come to Russia when she married Nicholas' uncle Grand Duke Serge Alexandrovich. Therefore, when Nicholas and Alexandra married, her sister became her aunt and her husband's uncle became her brother-in-law.

48 Judge Sergeyev felt that when he saw the victims at Alapayevsk that they were all victims of the same Ural Soviet that killed the Ekaterinburg victims.

49 Sir Charles reports that he supposes that the only victims in the house were the Tsar and the four attendants, again disputing Sokolov's conclusions.

50 Gilliard, Pierre. *Thirteen Years at the Russian Court*, Hutchinson & Company, London, 1923.

51 Telberg, George. *The Last Days of the Romanovs*, George H. Doran Company, New York, p. 15.

52 Ackerman, Carl W. *Trailing the Bolsheviki: Twelve Thousand Miles with the Allies in Siberia (1919)*, Charles Scribner's Sons, New York, 1919

53 Nicholas states that he decided to give Chemodurov a rest and that he took on Trupp as his replacement.

54 Alexandra's diary states that Chemodurov left as he was not feeling well.

55 Alexandra's diary, p. 198. The last entry in Alexandra's diary ends at 10:30 on July 16, 1918.

56 Volkov. *Memories of Alexei Volkov*. Translated to French by E. Semenov, Payot, Paris, 1928; translated to English by Robert Moshein, 2004.

57 Smythe, James P. *Rescuing the Tsar*. This printing by Tutis Publishing, Chennai, India 2007.

58 The reference here is to Parafine Domino where the other spelling in the Ackerman/Slaughter document names him Parfen Dominin. This book does contain the only mention to Domnin found anywhere else other than Ackerman.

59 Graves, Dr. Armgaard Karl. *The Secrets of the German War Office*, McBride, Nast and Company, New York, 1914.

60 The first Lord of the Admiralty was Winston Churchill from 1911 to 1915. At that point Churchill made a disastrous decision for an attack at Gallipoli, as a result of which he resigned his cabinet post.

61 Richard Haldane, First Viscount Haldane, was a Secretary of State for War from 1905 to 1912 and then served in the cabinet as Lord Chancellor from 1912 to 1915.

62 Wilton, Robert. *The Last Days of the Romanovs*, edition used was published in May 1993, following a British edition in 1920, a United States edition in 1920, a French edition published in Paris in 1921, and lastly a Russian edition published in Berlin in 1923. Readers did not understand that Wilton had assembled his book from Sokolov's report and, therefore, it was not an additional original report but basically a copy of Sokolov.

63 Mr. Bernstein, as we had noted, was deeply involved in investigating the Romanov murders and his review of Wilton's book is extremely critical.

64 Wilton, Robert. *The Last Days of the Romanovs*, p. 153. This statement by Weber appears in his introduction on Page XII and other text on page 153.

65 Wilton, p. 95

66 Wilton, p. 114

67 Wilton, p. 82

68 Wilton, p. 84

69 Alexandra Tegleva, known to the family as Shura, had been a nurse maid to the young daughters and also to Alexei. She went with the family to Tobolsk and stayed with the daughters and Alexei when the first group went to Ekaterinburg. She went to Ekaterinburg with the second group but was not allowed to leave the train. The Bolsheviks told her she was free to go but had to leave Ekaterinburg. She eventually made her way to France where she later married the tutor, Pierre Gilliard.

70 McNeal, Shay. *The Secret Plot to Save the Tsar: The Truth Behind the Romanov Mystery*, Harper Collins, New York, 2001.

71 Lockhart, R.H. Bruce. *British Agent*, G.P. Putnam's Sons, New York and London, 1933.

72 Francis, David Rowland. *Russia from the American Embassy, April, 1916 – November, 1918*, Charles Scribner's Sons, New York, 1921.

73 The obituary appears in <u>Assembly</u>, a West Point publication, and identifies Homer Havron Slaughter as Class of 1908 and died December 21, 1953 at Washington, D.C., aged 68 years.

74 Slaughter, Stephen S. *History of a Missouri Farm Family*, Harbor Hill Books, Harrison, New York, 1978.

75 Stephen Slaughter gave an oral history to the Truman Presidential Library on April 9, 1984. Truman Presidential Library, 500 W. U.S. Highway 24, Independence, Missouri 64050.

76 King, Gregory and Wilson, Penny. *The Fate of the Romanovs*, John Wiley & Sons, Hoboken, NJ, 2003.
    For general discussion of Halliburton's conversations with Ermakov, see page 19.

77 King, Gregory and Wilson, Penny. *The Fate of the Romanovs*, John Wiley & Sons, Hoboken, NJ, 2003, p.116.

78 Gilliard, Pierre. *Thirteen Years at the Russian Court*, Hutchison & Company, Paternoster Raw 3d edition, London, 1923, p. 277.

79 Summers, Anthony and Mangold, Thomas. *The File on the Tsar*, Harper & Row, New York, 1976, page 106, part 3, "The Suspect Telegram."

80 The victims were Grand Duke Serge, Grand Duchess Ella, Grand Duke Paul's morganatic son, and the three princes of the royal blood who were sons of Grand Duke Constantine.

81 Volkov, Alexei. *Memories of Alexei Volkov*. Translated to French by E. Semenov, Payot, Paris, 1928; translated to English by Robert Moshein, 2004.

82 McCullagh, Francis. *A Prisoner of the Reds, the Story of a British Officer Captured in Siberia*, John Murray, Albemarle St., W.1, London, 1921, pgs. 146-152. McCullagh says that he had occasion to visit Yurovsky at his home in 1920, and describes him as an aged man, shuffling about the house in pajamas and slippers. He indicates that Yurovsky is a ruined shadow of his former self. McCullagh believes that to be an effect of his participation in the murders.

83 Radzinsky, Edvard. *The Last Tsar*, Doubleday, New York, 1992.

84 Richards, Guy. *The Hunt for the Czar*, Doubleday & Company, Inc., Garden City, NY, 1970.

ABOUT THE AUTHOR

T. G. Bolen attended undergraduate and graduate school, majoring in history, and then received a law degree in 1960, all from the University of Illinois. He retired after fifty years in active practice as the senior partner of Bolen, Robinson, & Ellis, and he now devotes his full time to writing. Mr. Bolen has written on historical nonfiction subjects, primarily those taking place in the nineteenth and twentieth century, such as Custer's Last Stand at Little Bighorn and the US Army court martials and the subsequent executions of American soldiers in Europe in World War II.

CPSIA information can be obtained
at www.ICGtesting.com
Printed in the USA
BVHW081920171218
535790BV00009B/736/P